From the best-selling author of
Seeds of Greatness and
The Psychology of Winning

SAFARI TO THE SOUL

A GUIDE TO SURVIVAL, SUCCESS AND SERENITY IN THIS SAVAGE PARADISE CALLED LIFE

Denis Waitley

Published by: International Learning Technologies, Inc.
A Denis Waitley Company

Distributed by: YourSuccessStore.com

ISBN : 978-1-4243-4019-4

Printed in the United States of America

First Edition

Book design by Heather L. King

DEDICATION

To the Maasai and the Wildlife of the Mara
In the beginning, The Maestro created the land and all life,
to coexist and flourish in harmony. May those that follow
honor that maxim.

To my Children and Grandchildren
There is no greater joy and privilege than to be your Dad
and Papa for as long as I may live.

Acknowledgments

My appreciation to Calvin and Louise Cottar. Your vision for the future of the land and people you cherish will live on for generations. Thank you for protecting, creating, and nurturing the environment to make the word "safari" mean "coming home."

Thanks to our guide, lifelong friend, my buddy and my brother John Sampeke, who gave life and meaning to the words on the pages that follow.

A special acknowledgement to my colleague—Heather King—the designer and managing editor of this work, who turned a scribbled diary into a work that I feel is worthy as my literary legacy.

TABLE OF CONTENTS

FOREWORD

I didn't plan to write this book. I didn't ponder with a focus group, agent or publisher on how to produce a blockbuster bestseller. Material reward was not a motivating factor. This book just happened. In a way, it wrote itself. I feel more like its traveling companion than its author.

There are three milestones, however, that linked together to create the environment for this personal journey:

- My childhood fantasies
- Early interactions with my children
- An epiphany

As a boy, growing up during the 40s and 50s in San Diego, California, my fifteen-cent admission fee to the Hillcrest and Roxy theaters on Saturday afternoons spawned my first stirrings of the call of the wild outdoors. (Actually, the movie ticket was a dime, which left a nickel for popcorn or candy.)

Our first weekly serving was usually Frank Buck's *Bring 'Em Back Alive* in grainy black and white film clips documenting the harrowing experiences of Frank Buck capturing dangerous African beasts and proudly displaying them in cages bound for Barnum & Bailey bigtops or the San Diego Zoo. Even then I felt a disquieting pang of sadness for the animals wrenched from their sprawling, lush homeland to become curiosities for our weekend entertainment.

Soon, however, my conscience was salved as *Tarzan of the Apes* swung into view with Boy, Jane and Cheetah the Chimp, in close pursuit. I may date myself by revealing that I saw them all: Buster Crabbe, Johnny Weismuller and Lex Barker in the hero's role. For my ten cents, Johnny Weismuller will always be the *real* Tarzan. After all, his Tarzan yell was the most authentic and who could fault his ability to outswim even the swiftest river crocodile or four-oared canoe filled with evil diamond poachers?

Maybe because Tarzan's vocabulary was so limited: "Tarzan go. Boy stay. No follow. Mind Jane!" I yearned for increasingly imaginative adventures with more colorful and realistic dialogue. To this day, I am convinced that my orange public library card was a hundred times more valuable in my character development than anything I have ever purchased with my orange Mastercard. What kind of price can you assign to the vicarious thrills unfolding on the pages of Jack London, Herman Melville, Ernest Hemingway, C. S. Forester, James Michener and Isak Dinesen?

In my late teens, more African adventure movies filled the big screens and my fantasies of becoming an explorer or treasure hunter were once again stoked to exaggerated proportions. The remake of the 1937 film *King Solomon's Mines* in 1950—starring Deborah Kerr and Stewart Granger—cost me two weeks' of lunch money to see over and over again. In 1952, as I entered the U. S. Naval Academy at Annapolis, I eagerly thrust myself into the plot with Humphrey Bogart and Katherine Hepburn in *African Queen*, based upon the book I had read earlier by C. S. Forester. Africa was really put on the map as the ultimate in wildlife adventures in 1953, when Clark Gable, Ava Gardner and Grace Kelly starred in John Ford's technicolor extravaganza *Mogambo*.

And, as often happens with childhood dreams, my obsession in becoming a *National Geographic* editor, forest ranger or photo safari guide ended abruptly as I became a nuclear weapons delivery pilot catapulted off the deck of a U. S. Navy aircraft carrier somewhere in the Pacific Ocean. My fantasy of becoming a wildlife expert was replaced by the call to defend our freedom in the wild ride of supersonic steel in flight.

The second milestone leading to the inevitability of authoring this book occurred during the childhood years of my daughters and sons. Our favorite TV show was Mutual of Omaha's *Wild Kingdom*, featuring the wispy, lisping, but daring, Marlin Perkins. Marlin Perkins was a far cry from today's most popular wildlife character, Steve Irwin, The Crocodile Hunter, but that was a different era. (The good news is that "Wild

Kingdom" has been resurrected on television and my grandchildren and I are soaking it up together, which creates a strangely wonderful kind of dejas vu for me to revisit my cherished wildlife documentaries with the next generation.)

Our home was a virtual menagerie. Dogs and cats, hamsters and guinea pigs, bunnies, chickens, parakeets and turtles. Our malamute, Kheemo, ruined our beautiful flower garden and was furloughed to a sheep ranch in Wyoming. The hamsters escaped into the heating ducts in the floor. We heard the pitter-patter of little feet for weeks until a cold spell finally forced us to raise the thermostat. We still prefer to believe they escaped into the yard before the furnace came on. The cat dined on the parakeets. The bunnies multiplied so fast the pet store refused our offers to replenish their supply. And as happens to most small turtles, they were discovered upside down in the bottom of their grotto.

As the kids progressed into adolescence, the boys' fancies turned to contact sports and girls. The girls' attention graduated to horses and then later to boys. When my daughters were young teenagers, they shared my love for *National Geographic* specials and wildlife documentaries. Those many years ago, in the early 1970s, they asked me a simple but direct question: "Dad, we know how much you love wildlife, and you know how much we love wildlife. Will you ever take us on a safari to Africa so we can enjoy the animals in their natural habitat? We don't like the zoo, Dad! The animals there are like paranoid POWs with no hope for escape and no possibility of parole. Will you take us to Africa, Dad?"

"I promise, I will," I assured them with a hug, and went about my routine of earning our bread, watching TV and going to bed. Sunrise, sunset, year after year. Before I knew it

I was in my 60th-plus year. "Someday I must take them to Africa," I mused and another year passed unnoticed.

Over a twenty-year period, I have written fourteen non-fiction books. To me, a non-fiction, self-help book is "a term paper with an attitude!" Most of my books have been ruminating in my head for about six months prior to the actual writing. After outlining the chapters, with a clear concept of the central theme, I try to do the actual writing working for about 40 straight days and nights, putting in about 18 hours per sitting. Food and calls of nature are the only interruptions. I'm like a bear in hibernation with insomnia. As I write on my word processor, I like to listen to classical or semi-classical music. In the semi-classical vein, I love the epic movie soundtracks such as "Somewhere in Time", "Dances With Wolves," "The Last of the Mohicans," and "The Lion King."

By far the most inspirational CD soundtrack to spur my writing efforts is that from the movie *Out of Africa*. No doubt you saw the magnificent film starring Meryl Streep and Robert Redford released in 1985. If you haven't read the book, it's a must for your permanent library.

Written under the pen name of Isak Dinesen, *Out of Africa*, published in 1937, was written by Karen Blixen who lived in Kenya from 1914 to 1931. It is her love letter to the country she called home for nearly twenty years and is one of the most exquisite accounts of the landscape of the Ngong hill country and the animals and people who inhabited it. Her command of the English language is incomparable and, when reading this book, I had to remember that I was reading prose instead of poetry, because of the majesty of her descriptions of the migrating herds and the characterizations of the native people who touched her life.

I listened over and over again to the soundtrack from *Out of Africa* and dreamed of Kenya, but the 1990s came and went. My boys and girls flew the nest, with children of their own. And we never went to Africa. But be careful what you promise your children when they are young. They never forget a promise, no matter how old they are or how old you become. You are parents all of your lives, not simply while your off-spring are under your roof.

The turn of the century arrived and I celebrated the dawning of the new millennium with my oldest daughter, Deborah and my brother, Damon, near the active volcano Kilauea on the big Island of Hawaii. I had taken my two sons Denis and Darren on a wildlife outing in Alaska the year before, and there was this nagging feeling that my next-eldest daughter, Dayna, the most avid animal lover in the family, was somehow being short-changed. "I will have to do something special for her birthday next August," I admonished myself, and promptly put the idea on layaway, reverting to the routine of coming and going, hurrying and scurrying, so ingrained in our society's lifestyle.

Then, the epiphany occurred. It was no doubt an act of Providence, and pre-ordained, but I didn't know it at the time. I was invited to give a keynote address for the Board of Trustees, key faculty and administration, and alumni and boosters of United States International University in San Diego, which has become Allante University. I had pursued doctoral studies there which had one of the most prestigious faculties in psychology and human behavior anywhere in America. My employer and mentor, Dr. Jonas Salk—developer of the first effective polio vaccine—had recommended the university, located in the Scripps Ranch area of San Diego County, because of visiting scholars like Viktor Frankl, Herb Otto, William Glasser, S. I. Hayakawa and Abraham Maslow who frequently lectured on campus.

After my keynote lecture, there was an auction with the proceeds going to a scholarship for a young female student from USIU's sister campus in Nairobi, Kenya. She attended the reception and dinner, and I was struck by her intelligence and eagerness to learn. The final prize was a week-long safari for two in the famed Maasai Mara in Kenya.

My antenna went up and I jumped into the bidding process as if I were an aristocratic art collector vying with all comers for a Renoir or

VanGogh original. I didn't care what the previous bid was, I signaled one hundred to five hundred dollars more. Of course I was the winning bidder, although it cost me much more than my fee for the speaking engagement. It was an absolute must for me. Here was an opportunity to help a young African student get a college education and, at the same time, achieve my boyhood dream of a safari to the richest wildlife area in the world. I would have sold my car and put another mortgage on my house for this obsession! And, I would be able to take my daughter, Dayna, with me as a special birthday present and the fulfillment of a childhood promise to her and to myself.

What I could not possibly have foreseen at the time was that this particular event would profoundly and completely alter my thinking and priorities for the remainder of my life. This would not just be another wonderful holiday excursion with lots of videos and photos to share with family and friends. This would be a once-in-a-lifetime journey to the very core of my own belief system.

So deeply emotional has been the impact on who I am and what I believe, that it has become an annual, spiritual pilgrimage that I hope to continue as long as I can travel, walk, look, listen and feel.

It seems rather odd that a man who has devoted most of his life writing about, lecturing and counseling others about success and fulfillment in the biggest cities, largest convention halls, crowded stadiums and arenas throughout the industrialized world, should find himself gaining his most meaningful insights about the enlightened life in a tent and on the savanna in the Kenya highlands of East Africa. Perhaps by being still and listening to my own heartbeat, as the only human sound emanating from the vastness of the Mara, I was able to hear the music and lyrics of my own soul—that inner center that each of us visits so rarely, if at all, in the hurried gridlock of our daily existence.

I sing this inner song for you, the reader, with the sincere desire that—when you close the book—you will smile, touch a loved one, slow the pace of your own journey down a bit, and feel more connected not only to the past and future, but to those priceless, simple treasures in the moment that have no purchase price. I am convinced, as I approach the Indian Summer of my own saga, that life is a collection of memories over a very brief time span. Sometimes we all get so caught up in reaching our material goals, we sprint to the finish line without noticing the landscape along the track.

I hope this humble offering will inspire you to indulge yourself with extra minutes and hours watching more sunsets, moon rises and to lie down in the tall grass feeling the breeze in your hair as you watch the clouds drifting by on their endless journey. Come with me to Africa, and I will show you what I mean.

X

PROLOGUE
FIRST NIGHT REFLECTIONS

Thoughts, in my tent...

No monuments of steel and glass

No golden arches or endless drone
of fossil-burning, mechanized human
ants crawling on concrete trails to
and from cookie-cutter cocoons

Searching for food, diversion
and meaning

Only vastness and silence of
the savanna ecosystem
as far as the naked eye can see
and ear can hear

Now and then the stillness rudely
interrupted by the piercing sounds
of clarion calling,
zebra's nervous barking,
lion's guttural proclamations
of royal presence and dominance

And the irritating bleating of
the endless procession of wildebeest
echoing the life and death struggle
and synergy of millennia upon millennia

In the Savage Paradise of Eden—
The Maasai Mara of Kenya
where our early ancestors migrated
with the herds

Coexisting in harmony with all other
living creations playing their part
In the Maestro's orchestra

Here in my tent
casting a ten-foot shadow on the
canvas, dancing in the August wind
illuminated by kerosene lantern

Armed with journal and pen,
guarded by a young Maasai warrior
standing just outside as my faithful sentry
throughout the eerie
East African night

I began to scribble recollections
and observations of this adventure—

My own, Safari to the Soul

CHAPTER ONE
THE SAFARI CALLED LIFE

Check-off list:

- ☐ Learn from those who have gone before
- ☐ Travel lightly; no extra baggage
- ☐ Be prepared and expect the unexpected
- ☐ The more you learn the less you fear
- ☐ Slow down, watch and listen
- ☐ Respect your environment
- ☐ Leave your ego behind
- ☐ Anticipate, innovate and make do
- ☐ Be optimistic; tomorrow did not exist before
- ☐ Collect memories instead of souvenirs
- ☐ Enjoy the journey
- ☐ Celebrate all life, not just your own

Kenya, arguably the original Eden, is humankinds' lost paradise, in which for thousands of years our ancestors dwelled in harmony with all living things, and thus with themselves. The Maasai Mara, where my safaris have been spent, is a combination of majesty and innocence, teeming with a variety of life—animals, birds, insects, plants and a few tribes' people. All of what can be called creation is there, living in the Maestro's natural order from which only industrialized, technology-savvy humans have disassociated themselves, by their confined, hurried life-styles complicated by the extra dimension of self-consciousness and self-importance they have assumed as their special privilege. In our modern society, humans are detached from their own past, far away from their natural heritage.

During my safaris, I soon realized that scribbled diaries, journals, photos and videos were but a feeble attempt to prove that I had visited this savage paradise, and could not begin to describe the past still alive in the present.

I thought I knew what to expect. Travel agents had briefed me in earnest. Friends related their own reflections of what they had seen in other parts of Africa. National Geographic and Discovery Channel specials had given me a glimpse of the Kenya terrain and its inhabitants. But nothing, really, prepares you for life in East Africa. No matter what is told about it, it retains an aura of the unknown, full of enigmas and misinterpretations. Mundane questions belie our ignorance: "What about the heat?" What inoculations do I need and what about quinine for malaria?" "What about terrorist activity from Somalia?" "What about the lions?" "Can you be dragged from your tent by a marauding beast and eaten during the night?"

I soon realized that my safari camp was safer and more secure than downtown in any city back home. Certainly, knowledge, preparation and choosing the right safari company are important. When I speak of what I expected upon arrival, I am not referring to logistics and security. It is the awesome, emotional impact of the experience.

> Nothing can prime you for East Africa. It is too overwhelming, both in scope and activity—a spectrum of life so much broader and more vivid than anywhere else in the world, that it seems to require a new set of senses, or the rediscovery of dormant ones buried deep in our subconscious minds like dinosaur fossils.

Many authors, myself included, have written books about success being more associated with the journey than the destination. We caution that rather than being obsessed with a trophy on the wall or a bouquet of roses in the winner's circle as the ultimate payoff, we would all be better off to appreciate the diversity of nature and our own role in maintaining harmony and synergy, and smell the fragrance of the roses along the way. My trips to Kenya have etched this wisdom deep into the very core of my soul.

A myopia shared by most people living in the developed countries is our obsession with goal achievement in our own private pursuits, which often obscures the beauty of the landscape around us. We fret and hurry as if life were a race to reach the finish line first, rather than an experience to savor and make last. We spend the majority of our lives seeking tangible, material proof that our own lives are significant and special in comparison to others.

> To live a life of significance, it may be wise to relish and marvel at our individual insignificance compared to the incredible, natural symphony that the maestro, our creator, has orchestrated all around us.

The Maasai Mara in Kenya is a world and way of life from which one returns transformed. Back home, nothing is as it was before and everything is viewed from a totally different perspective. We often hear about "moments of truth," "flashes of insight," and "instant religion." To spend only a few days in this savage paradise is to lose your old identity and begin to create a new one. This is what can happen when you subordinate yourself to your surroundings completely, so they are no longer separate from you but become part of you for the remainder of your life.

I prefer to view life as a way of traveling on a mysterious, ever-challenging safari, where the trail to heaven or hell is blazed by our daily, hourly and minute-by-minute choices, actions and responses. The word *safari*, has roots in ancient Arabic language, and has come to mean "pertaining to a journey". I am using my brief experiences in East Africa to

4

expand the meaning of *safari* as a journey into enlightenment that each of us takes to comprehend the richness and legacy of our own existence.

Many in the industrialized nations become seduced into believing that the terms "standard of living" and "quality of life" are synonymous. In my opinion, there is a difference as large as the continent of Africa itself.

> *Standard of living is the amount of money you have to spend. Quality of life is how you spend your time.*

Beyond certain basics, the two terms are poles apart in meaning. Success, courtesy of Hollywood, Madison Avenue, MTV and ESPN, is usually associated with celebrity, wealth and hedonism. Reality television is truly a fashion statement on immediate sensual gratification and indulgence. We seem to be obsessed with values described by the ultimate oxymoron: *skin-deep*. Our preoccupation with bizarre, stylistic and provocative behavior results in an almost total eclipse of insight, intimacy and cultural sharing. Rather than fashion imitating life, life is imitating fashion in the 21st century. It appears that we have learned little from the past as history keeps repeating itself as surely as the great herds of East Africa repeat their annual migration in search of food and water.

The ancient pharaohs of Egypt were similarly preoccupied, and wasted thousands of lives and generations of their loyal subjects, building the great pyramids that would not only demonstrate the leaders' great power as far as the eye could see, but also securely store their accumulated riches for their journey in the afterlife. They had never been introduced to the "you can't take it with you" concept and narcissistically bought into the idea that they could even utilize the same body, when carefully embalmed and mummified, the second time around.

The search for everlasting youth is like a mirage on a hot, arid plain disguised as a pool of potable drinking water. Our thirst for it plays tricks on our eyes. Youth and success are states of mind, and should be viewed from inside out, as soul-deep rather than skin-deep values. In our modern society, we crave immortality in the physical sense. With notions, potions and lotions; with lasers, scalpels and vacuum cleaners, we cut, polish, nip and tuck, inject and suck any signs of age from our aging bodies in a futile attempt to defy gravity and time.

> Back home you believe you can fool Mother Nature. On safari in East Africa, you realize you cannot. Surrounded by the most abundant and diverse life still existing on earth, you are equally surrounded by the reality of mortality.

The struggle for life and death is everywhere in Africa. If the zebra had turned right instead of left, it would still be alive. If the wildebeest had crossed the Mara river a half hour earlier, the crocodiles would not have had such a feast. What is true in the natural kingdom also holds true in our own civilized world. Life, everywhere, is a gift and forever subject to choice and chance, as it is to the endless cycles of bud, bloom, blossom and seed. If he hadn't driven on that freeway at that moment he'd still be living. It they had not boarded that plane, or entered that building, or made that choice, things would be different. "If onlys" and "could haves" linger in human hindsight and cloud our perspective.

Returning from safari, I felt I could accept anything, including my own mortality. That's how profound the experience was for me and can be for you, if you have yet to get out of your comfort zone and into the Maasai Mara of Kenya.

Success in most cultures, certainly in our own, has been associated with material wealth, fame and social status. I call our preoccupation with showing others the fortunes we've built—the Edifice Complex. Many people try to emulate the pharaohs, spending their lives erecting monuments to their progress. As their lives draw to a close there often is a stark reality check in the revelation that collecting memories was more important than collecting money or status symbols. More than likely the latter are squabbled over by competing heirs or auctioned at garage sales at ten cents on the dollar.

> *One of the most important lessons I have learned in my own life is that the precious time I have spent with my family is priceless compared to the inordinate amount of money I spent on them. What you leave in your children's hearts and minds is infinitely more important than what you leave to your children in your estate.*

Taking my own children and grandchildren to Africa on safari ranks among the peak experiences in all of my life. I would not trade those special days and nights for all the material fortunes and celebrity status that are the envy of the masses. If you asked my kids and grandkids, I'm certain they would agree.

When you come to Africa on safari, leave your satellite cell phone and laptop at home. Don't bring your briefcase full of incomplete work projects. Pack lightly. And, above all, don't do what most tourists do. Don't overschedule and overplan.

> *It's not how many photos you can show your friends and family. It is watching, listening and becoming one with the terrain and its inhabitants.*

Simplify your itinerary. Take the time to become part of the surrounding environment. It's not a question of how much you can cram into a day or a week. Slow down and become aware of your senses. Observe the wonders you are beholding. A safari is not a race. It is making time stand still and discovering what's really significant in this journey called life. If you do it right, you will be transformed as I and my family have been.

CHAPTER TWO
THE COTTARS' 1920s SAFARI CAMP

I mentioned that I had no idea what to expect in East Africa. This also was true concerning the safari package I had purchased at an auction as a benefit for a young Kenyan student. All I knew was that Calvin and Louise Cottar had donated a week-long safari for two persons at their camp in the Maasai Mara region of Kenya as part of a scholarship fund for the University of Nairobi.

I selected the last week in August for the trip to coincide with my daughter Dayna's birthday on August 25th. It was as a special present I had promised her since she was nine years old, several decades before. When my eldest daughter, Deborah, learned of her sister's good fortune, she used her well-developed power of persuasion, that no father can resist, to invite herself to join us, reminding me that I had promised to take the entire family to Africa as well. Soon the party increased to a total of five. Two daughters, two sons-in-law and dad. I smiled to myself with the understanding that, upon our return, my other children would be on my case for equal time, along with a bevy of grandchildren, many of whom are reaching an age where they can remember and appreciate that kind of magnificent feast for the eyes. And so it has become an annual pilgrimage for our family. As long as dad is coherent, ambulatory and has enough frequent flyer miles accumulated, another Cottars' 1920s safari is scheduled.

I have been blessed with unbridled optimism, unending curiosity, mostly positive outcomes and an inordinate quantity of good luck. I could not have been luckier in being the winning bidder for the Cottars' Safari.

Until our party arrived at the camp, I had no idea that Cottar is the longest serving name in the African safari business, with more than 80 years of experience handed down through the generations. The Cottar Safari tradition began in 1919 by Charles Cottar, who was joined in the family business by his sons, Bud, Mike and Ted during the 20s, 30s and 40s.

At the end of my first safari, I did some belated homework concerning the family and learned from the classic book, *White Hunters*, that the Cottar clan is referred to as the "first family of the safari business." Reading about Charles Cottar is like revisiting the likes of Teddy Roosevelt. In his prime, Charles stood well over six feet tall, was muscular and fearless, with a pioneering spirit found mostly in astronauts and polar explorers in this millennium. He was the essence of an "outdoor man" with great strength and dauntless courage who, after being mauled more than once by a leopard, strangled one with his bare hands and wore the testimony of those events as visible scars and a paralyzed left side.

The earliest Cottars introduced many innovations to the safari industry that are taken for granted today. They were the first to use motor vehicles on safari, first to make a color film in Africa, and probably the first to tame an orphaned cheetah, leopard, wild dog, chimpanzee and striped hyena as pets. They guided and supported some of the most famous safari expeditions ever undertaken for George Eastman, Martin and Olsa Johnson, the Duke and Duchess of York and the Queen Mother of England.

During the 50s, 60s and 70s, the camp was operated by Mike's son Glen and his wife, Pat. In 1964, the Cottars established the first permanent tented tourist camp in Africa in Tsavo Park. Since the 1990s, the Cottar legacy has been maintained and upgraded by Glen's son Calvin and his wife, Louise. With the development of their one-of-a-kind tented safari camp, they have earned the reputation as the finest, most authentic, most atmospheric and ecologically-correct adventure re-creating the glamour and style of a classic safari of yesteryear.

Through the decades, the Cottar family sadly observed that the quality of safaris in Kenya had generally deteriorated as operators sacrificed raw excitement for convenience, tour groups and budgets. In many instances safaris have become over-itinerized, limited to congested, big-name parks, barracks and cafeteria style, with caravans of minivans and microbuses chasing each other over well-traveled dirt roads for a glimpse and photo-op of lion, giraffe, or elephant at a distance of 30 to 200 meters.

As our well-equipped, mostly-new, all-wheel-drive vehicles, courtesy of Cottars, navigated even the most uninviting and treacherous terrain—sometimes 50 to 100 miles from camp—we were often interrogated by the drivers of overcrowded microbuses and minivans confined to the beaten paths: "Have you seen any lions today?" Our personal guide would smile and recommend a secure vantage point a mile down the road where a good pair of binoculars or a zoom lens would bring them comfortably into view.

Out of courtesy, he never mentioned that we had been sitting quietly for the past hour in the midst of a pride of nineteen lions teasing the cubs with a rope less than a meter away, as if we were playing with kittens and a spool of thread. Since we traveled where no minivans can go, we did not flaunt our good fortune in being able to disappear into the Mara as if we were part of the migrating herds themselves.

Our game drives couldn't have been more thrilling and our walks and hikes were like nothing we have ever experienced before or since. There are many outstanding safari companies serving the Maasai Mara Game Reserve that offer walking or tented excursions and excellent game driving outings. For me and my family, however, the Cottars' camp was so unique and special that we talk about it every time we assemble for a holiday or reunion and can't wait to schedule a return visit.

It is patently clear that the Cottars aren't in this business for the money. While it is notable that they were declared the Best Small Business in the African Tourism sector and overall East African winner for Best Business in Africa at the first Africa SMME Awards' function held in Johannesburg, South Africa recently, based upon financial soundness, quality, integrity, social responsibility and community development, you need to meet the Cottars in person to understand their motivation.

> *Calvin and Louise Cottar are preserving and nurturing their preferred way of life in the land that they cherish. This is not an enterprise to them, it is their essence.*

According to *Travel and Leisure* magazine, the Cottars are the "Kennedys of the East African safari industry". It didn't take me more than ten minutes in our initial face-to-face meeting to understand the comparison. I immediately knew why they don't need gratuitous press and travel agent junkets to attract paying customers. Their newsworthiness is self-perpetuated by the guests upon their return home.

Calvin and Louise Cottar are in a word, unforgettable. Calvin is tall, lean and ruggedly handsome, with quiet confidence and a disarming ability to greet you for the first time as if you were a long lost friend. Louise is radiantly beautiful, gracious and warm, with an artistic, creative touch that can be seen and felt in every aspect of the authentic 1920s camp, which the couple developed themselves as their personal signatures to the longstanding family commitment to wildlife conservation.

Forgive me for gushing so exuberantly about the Cottars. They are not even aware I am mentioning them in this book and they will no doubt be embarrassed or even a bit irritated by my unsolicited praise. However, consider the circumstances. Like myself, you may have been the successful high bidder at a charity auction offering a getaway vacation to some exotic place and took it for granted that it would be special. Without further investigation, I escorted my daughters on a surprise birthday outing. The only research I undertook was how best to travel and what to bring. I was so excited making our airline reservations I didn't even bother to investigate the Cottars' Web site other than to go down the list of suggested clothing. The rule of thumb for a safari in Kenya is the less you pack, the more enjoyable the trip. (Being one of America's most frequent fliers over a 30-year period I thought I was traveling smart and light until I arrived at the camp with my Louis Vitton hanging bag,leather duffel bag and carry-on, only to discover that the Cottars provide daily laundry service even in the wild). I had even forgotten to pack Woolite with my seven pair of Calvin Klein underwear!

All you really need are some casual clothes for warm days (70 to 80 degrees) and cool nights (40 to 60 degrees), good hiking boots or walking shoes, tee shirts, socks, underwear, a hat, camera, binoculars and a soft duffel bag for your clothes, weighing no more than 33 pounds when packed and a carry-on case for toiletries and camera.

So what I'm saying is that, by serendipity, I wandered into the premier tented safari experience without anticipating it. When I reflect, I shudder to think that we could just as easily have been stuffed in a minivan with an impatient, Type-A tour group from New York, who were spending one day and a night in six different lodges, hoping to video the "big five" game animals from a hot air balloon, and never would have known the difference. How many vacation locations have you found that you would return to every year for a week for the rest of your life? Not many, I'll wager. That is why meeting Calvin and Louise Cottar was such a delightful bonus.

Calvin, a fourth generation Kenyan, grew up in the bush learning from his father, Glen, and Bajila, his father's tracker. As a young teenager, Calvin started his wildlife career guiding clients on game drives and walks from the family lodge in the Mara. He spent five years as a professional hunter in Tanzania and returned to Kenya to establish a wildlife management company providing services to landowners in the region. In 1993, he joined the Kenya Wildlife Service initiating five district wildlife associations to help landowners acquire user rights of their wildlife. In 1995, Calvin rejoined the family company to create the 1920s tented safari project.

Louise Cottar, a native of England, first came to Kenya in 1989 while pursuing graduate studies in international business. After receiving her master's degree she had several professional assignments in Europe and returned to Africa permanently in 1994. A pioneer and adventuress in her own right, Louise undertook a daring assignment as coordinator for a special United Nations program in Somalia, one of the most unstable and dangerous countries in which to live and work, especially for a young woman. She has earned her reputation for excellence and ingenuity while never flinching in the face of considerable personal risk. To those who know her well, Louise can be likened to a modern-day Karen Blixen, the autobiographer of *Out of Africa*.

Commuting from their family compound in the Karen suburb of Nairobi (named after Karen Blixen), the Cottars spend much of their time at their 1920s camp and their Bushtops homestead in the Maasai Mara. The two adolescent Cottar sons, Danni and Jasper, eagerly anticipate their holidays from Pembroke House, an outstanding boarding school in Gilgil, a town in the Rift Valley of Kenya. It's not unusual to see them on a game drive or hike, with their father displaying the inimitable instincts of expert spotters and trackers inherent in their bloodlines and upbringing.

On my last Cottars'safari, I was pleasantly surprised to meet the Cottars' infant daughter, Charlie, the cutest potential "tomboy in lace" I have ever encountered, who seemed quite at home in the bush. I can hardly wait to see the changes in her and her baby sister, since Charlie will be nearly 3 years of age at the date of publication of this book and her little sister, Ella Tana, will be just about ready to replace crawling with her first steps on her own when I return for my next safari with more of my children.

At the beginning of our very first safari, my family and I had spent the night in the Hotel Serena in Nairobi after our long flights from the United States to Kenya so that we could be better rested and acclimated for the adventure ahead. We expected the forty-minute commuter flight to the Mara to be uneventful—not realizing that we were entering a world so foreign to our previous experience that we soon stopped chatting and laughing and focused our attention on the terrain below. Within the first five minutes of the flight, houses seemed to vanish completely as if an earthquake or flood had swept them all away. We went from urban to rural in almost the blink of an eye.

It seemed like we were looking down at the surface of a strange planet combining aspects of the moon, Mars, Utah, Nevada, Arizona or Texas, and devoid of human population. It looked like parched California or Australia backcountry six months after wildfires had swept through.

> *It is impossible to put into words, your first impressions of the plains of East Africa, even from a small porthole in a commuter aircraft. It was as if we were leaving the world we knew and were entering a lost continent, a real-life Jurassic Park.*

I squinted at barren hills, canyons and gorges, unusually shaped trees, patches of red-clayed earth, indigo mountains in the background, stretches of amber and green grassland, scrub bushes of every configuration, winding rows of trees snaking along old river beds and tributaries, and dark shadows caused by slowly moving cloud formations above. Or were they shadows?

Upon closer examination, the shadows became herds of elephant. And what were all those thousands of columns of ants doing there? They had four legs and horns. But the sheer numbers made them seem like millions of ants. Were they really wildebeests? How could there be so many of them and so much of everything? With binoculars, I could distinguish the buffalo, zebra, and giraffe from what appeared to the naked eye to be simply herds of cattle.

From Calvin Cottar's first handshake, as we deplaned at the Keekorok Airstrip, the closest commercial landing strip to our destination, I could understand why he has been voted the best wildlife guide in

Kenya. As we piled into his Land Rover, he casually mentioned that there was a good chance we would encounter some very interesting sights on our two-hour drive to the camp, whereupon he promptly went through the gears and veered straight off the red dirt road into the savanna.

I could not imagine attempting to rent an off-road vehicle and make that trek, even with the most sophisticated global positioning satellite system on board. Without road signs or clearly distinguishable roads, and no compass, what do you use for landmarks? Acacia trees? Unusually shaped boulders? Erosion cracks in the earth?

I soon forgot these questions as we suddenly came upon a magnificent mother cheetah and two young cubs resting in the shade. Turning off the ignition, Calvin coasted our vehicle to within five feet of the beautiful cats and we spent the next twenty minutes, in the first of hundreds of similar situations, introducing ourselves to an intimacy with wildlife impossible in any zoo or wild animal park anywhere in the world. The absence of fear and the nonchalance with which they accepted us made us realize that we were simply passersby and part of the landscape in their natural habitat.

What a marvelous animal the cheetah is to behold. If lion is the "king of beasts," then surely the cheetah is the "beast of kings." The ancient Asyrian kings groomed the cheetah's ancestors as pets and hunters. Hooded, like falcons, these royal cats were led out into the field and let loose to fetch deer or gazelle for their masters.

> *It was like reconnecting with stirrings inside of me that had been caged and fettered, almost forgotten completely throughout my life. It was the beginning of a new identity for me, where the past and present seemed indistinguishable from each other. I wondered if my children were experiencing these same emotions, but we all were too involved in the moment to utter a word. We simply sat in silence and watched.*

Our mother cheetah, although smaller than the full-grown males we would see later in our safari, looked like an oversized, muscular greyhound, dressed in a leopard skin, except for the long black line leading from the corner of each eye down to her chin, as if tears had left a black streak. The dark tear marks beneath the eyes may also enhance its visual acuity by minimizing the sun's glare. We discussed the fact that many professional football and baseball players sometimes put black grease paint under their eyes to reduce the sun's glare and wondered whether a coach or trainer fashioned that idea after observing cheetahs.

Cheetahs are unique among the many cat species. With a head that seems too small for its body, and with small teeth more canine than feline, its paws too, are almost dog-like. Narrow and hard padded they sport only slightly-retractable claws, unlike other cats in the wild, which aid in gripping the terrain like track shoes on an Olympic sprinter.

When you look at a cheetah, you think to yourself, "built for speed." Virtually every part of its anatomical design is adapted in some way to maximize running speed which can reach about 70 miles per hour over distances normally not exceeding 300 yards. Calvin Cottar pointed out the features of the long, fluid body streamlined over light bones with its spine serving as a spring for its powerful back legs to give it added reach for each step. Small collarbones and vertical shoulder blades aid in lengthening the stride, with the long tail acting as a rudder to facilitate quick turns. Her large nostrils and lungs provide quick air intake and a large liver, heart and adrenals make possible rapid physical response.

Again, unlike most big cats, the cheetah does not roar, however it does purr and its other vocal sounds range from high pitched yelps and barks to chirping sounds, especially when she is communicating with her cubs. She can even mimic some bird sounds, perhaps to attract them. Uncharacteristic of felines, she hunts mainly by day, usually stalking her prey from a distance, which is enhanced by the eye's retinal fovea having an elongated shape, giving the cheetah a sharp, wide-angle view of its surroundings. The cheetahs' diet consists mainly of small antelope including springbok, steenbok, duikers, impala and Thompson's gazelle. These antelope can run faster than any animal except a cheetah, capable of speeds up to 50 miles per hour.

After a successful hunt, because the speed involved is very physiologically taxing, she will often pause to regain her strength before eating. At this time she and her prey are especially vulnerable to other predators and she can lose her meal to lions, hyenas and to other scavengers of the open plains. Adult male relatives usually travel in groups with much larger territories than the lone female hunter we were observing, who must stay close to her young. Cheetah cubs, between two and four to a litter, have a poor survival rate, commonly falling victim to lions or hyenas. After about eighteen months following and learning from their mother, the young cheetahs are ready to fend for themselves.

As we drove away and headed toward camp, Calvin soberly admitted that due to human influence and encroachment, the cheetahs' range has shrunken dramatically and their numbers dwindled. He suggested that in the not-to-distant future, sightings in the wild could become as rare as the tigers of Asia, snow leopards and rhinos. We stared back through our binoculars framing the family of three as if we might never have a close encounter like that ever again in our lifetimes.

My first major revelation on the journey happened just then, before we ever arrived at our destination where the safari would begin. I thought to myself that humans did not weave the web of life. With the arrogance of monarchs, we fashion ourselves as superior to all other creatures in the Maestro's orchestra, yet each of us is only a strand in the web, the delicate circle of life. With each species of wildlife that becomes extinct, a part of us dies as well. In West Africa, the elephants of Timbuktu are the only large mammals remaining in the region. What we do to the web, we do to ourselves.

CHAPTER THREE
SOMEWHERE IN TIME

It was deep purple dusk when we crossed the last stream bed and made the final incline to the entrance of the camp. We were still subdued and awestruck from the sights and sounds of the past two hours on our trek from the airstrip, having come upon herds of elephants, giraffe, zebra and, of course, literally hundreds of wildebeests trampling and zigzagging back and forth in the path of our Land Rover.

The outdoor camp lanterns—already lit for the evening—cast dancing shadows against the stark whiteness of the tents. A fire had been started in the fire pit, with canvas and wood director chairs placed around it in a circle awaiting the arrival of the other guests, who soon would be returning from their afternoon game drives. It was a nightly ritual to share new experiences over gourmet hors d'ouvres served on silver trays, accented by a glass of vintage South African wine served in crystal glasses. This was "roughing it" for elitists in the 1920s. Parked just above us was an eight-passenger, vintage Rolls Royce, open roof, wood-paneled safari touring car, looking as if it had just been uncrated after its long steamship voyage from England, ready to squire the Royal Family on a game drive.

As the guides, trackers and staff eagerly welcomed our arrival, I had a visual and emotional flashback as if I had passed through a time warp to an old but familiar place. Was this really happening or fantasy? Would I awaken in my bed in California wondering about the vividness of what was surely just a mirage?

While my daughters and sons-in-law exchanged greetings and unloaded our gear, I stood transfixed in my dream world as my thoughts raced back a number of years to another scene that had evoked similar emotions within me. It was fall of the year 2000 and I was a keynote speaker for an event that coincided with the 20th annual celebration of the motion picture, *Somewhere in Time*, filmed on location at the Grand Hotel on the Straits of Mackinac waterfront in Michigan, and first released in 1980.

Based upon a novel by Richard Matheson, the original setting was supposedly the famed Hotel Del Coronado, only a stone's throw from my home near San Diego. It is my understanding that the Grand Hotel was chosen for the film because the immediate areas around the old Del Coronado are too modern and commercial to create the overall nostalgia sought in the story. Along with *Out of Africa*, *Somewhere in Time* and its musical soundtrack are among my all-time favorites and I felt honored to participate in the 20th anniversary, in the company of two of my favorite artists, Christopher Reeve and Jane Seymour.

The festival features period costumes, the showing of the movie, and a partial re-enactment of some of the most memorable scenes. As Christopher Reeve, in his special wheelchair with life support equipment, was brought into the hotel, my heart swelled with admiration for his courageous example of treating tragedy as a mere inconvenience in his life. If you saw the film, you may recall that Christopher assumes the role of Richard Collier, a successful Chicago playwright, who is approached by an old woman who alters his destiny. Handing him a classic pocket watch she whispers four haunting words "Come back to me," which will affect him forever. Eight years later, while visiting the Grand Hotel on Mackinac Island, young Richard Collier is mesmerized by a portrait of a lovely actress, Elise McKenna, who had been one of the first ladies of stage in 1912, played by Jane Seymour. So obsessed with her was Richard, that he discovered a purely, non-scientific method of time travel to transport himself backward nearly seventy years into her life. As heartbreaking as both *Somewhere in Time* and *Out of Africa* were to us the observers and as impossible as it was to leave either movie dry-eyed, we were inspired and reminded of the power of love and passion for life that transcend both time and space. I was enraptured by the similarities of the two events.

My daughters, Deborah and Dayna, nudged me back to reality, "Dad, are you okay?"

> *Here I was, in a way going back in time more than eighty years, with another four words whispered in my ear by the wind in the trees coming off an East African mountain: "You are home again." How could I be home again, if this was my first time here?*

"What, oh sure, I'm fine. I was just caught up in the realization that we are really here and wondering, at the same time, what took me so long to chase my passion," I shook my head as I slung my duffle back over my shoulder and followed them.

"Well, we're excited and glad you decided to share it with us. Thanks so much for the great birthday present, Dad," Dayna smiled.

Debi chimed in, "Yeah, and did you notice that 'Chitty-chitty-bang-bang' old car back there? It's like traveling through a time tunnel back to the 1920s, isn't it?"

As we approached the luxurious main tented compound, housing the dining room, lounging room, library and gift area, we were met by the owners.

In addition to the huge dining, lounging and library tents, there are six permanent tents, accommodating up to 12 clients in authentic, spacious white canvas structures, exquisitely furnished with original safari

Glancing at the total effect in re-creating safari life in the 20s, complete with tents, sofas, throw pillows, antique cabinetry, books, candelabras, Persian rugs, the old Victrola and records that surely must have been the original props used to depict Karen Blixen's house in Out of Africa, I halfway expected to see Meryl Streep and Robert Redford give us the tour to complete my Jane Seymour and Christopher Reeve illusion. Instead it was Louise and Calvin Cottar who showed our party the lay of the land and their labor of love.

antiques reminiscent of a golden, bygone era. Each guest tent, separated by distance and foliage to afford maximum privacy, features bedrooms with romantic four poster beds, ensuite dressing rooms, upgraded lighting systems, bathrooms with flushable toilets, solar powered hot water, old fashioned styled tubs, showers and verandahs with breathtaking views. I spent many hours during the next seven days lounging there outside my tent, on the lower slopes of a heavily forested hillside—at an altitude higher than Denver, Colorado—staring out at the green-blond Mara plains and Tanzania's Serengeti beyond, that seemed to go on forever.

Certainly the posh accommodations were more than anticipated. Massage, manicure, pedicure, laundry service, the finest food and drink elegantly prepared and served with china and silver, a swimming pool built out of natural rock, and a specially tailored safari plan catering to the desires of each guest or party, consisting of our own private guide, spotter and vehicle. The amenities are too numerous to mention.

But don't let me mislead you. This is no tourist stop. This also is not a Ritz Carlton or Hyatt Regency resort, with golf, tennis, or shuffle board; as it surely is not for those who are used to city buses and pack-aged group plans.

> While it is true that it is perhaps the ultimate in first class service and platinum treatment, it is not for sis-sies and stodgy urbanites. It may provide an ambience of aristocracy, however you need to bring along some sturdy walking shoes and plenty of stamina and nerve. It took me only one night alone in my tent to figure this out and remember our geographic location.

Because of the Cottar legacy and reputation, Calvin and Louise were able to locate the camp on a 250,000-acre exclusive concession in the Maasai Mara, away from anything we consider as civilization. There is literally nothing like it anywhere in the country. The area has been untouched by any kind of tourism or development. We rarely saw anyone on our game drives and hikes other than Maasai warriors, herdsmen or another vehicle from our own camp. About the only time we saw the others, in our total complement of twelve guests, was at breakfast and dinner and on our one-day trip to the Mara River to witness the wildebeest crossing.

> It was just what I had dreamed of: Africa, up-close, private and personal. Coming home, not just passing through. Participating, not checking off a travel agent's itinerary. Collecting memories, instead of souvenirs.

After the Cottars gave us the tour, and after meeting the other eight guests—two from England, two from Japan, two from Australia, and two from Mexico—my family and I decided to take our leave and disperse to our three tents.

> Curiously, I thought, we were escorted to our tents by a Maasai warrior with a spear in one hand and a lantern in the other. "What a nice gesture," I thought to myself. Or was it just a gesture?

I zippered up my tent entrance, noticing that the entire structure was completely secured with a canvas flooring that was attached to the sides.

Not a single bug or creepy crawler could enter my kingdom. It was very dark and very quiet, and I quickly illuminated my own lantern beside my bed. The bed was fully draped with gossamer mosquito netting, but totally unnecessary, since I don't recall seeing or hearing one in my quarters during the entire stay.

After showering, sliding into bed, and extinguishing the kerosene lamp—still feeling the effects of my time warp, out-of-body experience—I began to notice that all of my other senses were beginning to overcompensate for my sudden plunge into total darkness. I began to wish the tents weren't so private and far apart.

> I closed my eyes and tried to sleep, wondering why the Maasai warrior who accompanied me to my suite was carrying a spear. And why was he standing guard just outside? Or was he?

CHAPTER FOUR
THINGS THAT GO "BUMP" IN THE NIGHT

Fear is an interesting phenomenon. It may be caused or fueled by the imagination, but it is real to the person experiencing it. It is totally inappropriate to tell a child, for example, "There's nothing to be afraid of." And if you don't experience a tinge of fear during your first night in a tent in Africa, you simply are not alive or are lying to yourself.

I grew up in the glorious days of radio. Our primary source of family entertainment was to congregate, after supper, and listen to our favorite comedy or mystery shows in front of the huge Philco upright console, which was our major investment in furniture. As a result, fortunately or unfortunately, I am more auditory than visual, in that I don't need television or big screen images to give me a dry throat, rapid heart rate, a cold sweat or hyperventilation. My masochistic appetite for being scared out my wits as a child was sated by popular radio programs in the 1940s including *Inner Sanctum*, *Lights Out* and *The Whistler.*

You no doubt were weaned on horror movies like *Psycho, Halloween, Scream* or *The Texas Chainsaw Massacre*, but bear with me while I try to convince you that what you can't see, or don't see, can

Helpless in my tent, I found myself a child again in the inner sanctum, with the lights out, and, heard myself uncontrollably begin to whistle

raise bigger goose bumps than what you peek at through hand-covered eyes. The ear is more the trickster than the eye. And I was beginning to hear things that made me wish my mom and dad were here again, with their reassuring inspection of my closet, the windows and especially checking under my bed for monsters and ghosts I was certain were there.

The inside of my tent became part of the utter darkness outside. I stared into a velvet blanket of solid blackness with wide eyes that saw nothing. Then the noises began. First there were the unmistakable sounds of lions roaring. How close were they? I knew sound traveled far and distance was deceptive without the barriers of concrete and steel. The roaring seemed no more than 50, 20 or even 10 yards away. "Do they know I'm here? Are they hungry?" I thought.

The top of my tent and the sides began to undulate with tapping and scratching from every side. Baboons began to cry out, no doubt sending the alarm that *simba* was ready to swipe a giant clawed paw through my puny canvas walls, grab me by the throat and drag me off into the thicket. I could hear the warnings of zebras barking and the bleating of wildebeests. As with anyone who is sight-impaired, my auditory senses became more acute. I was certain I could hear the breathing and silent padded approach of some giant predator prowling out there only a few feet from my pillow. I re-ignited my kerosene lantern, tried to read for a while, and wrote the prologue prose for this book.

"This is lunacy," I chastised myself. "I'm a Sean Connery-type of senior citizen who used to get his kicks flying a supersonic jet off an aircraft carrier in bad weather!" I turned the lamp off in a final gesture of mocked courage.

> In the darkness again, I attempted to will myself into a state of calmness and serenity. Instead of counting sheep, I tried counting wildebeest.

But there I lay, the macho man, scarcely breathing, immobilized. To this day I am unsure whether or not I slept at all, until I was rescued by the gray light of dawn. My anxious passage through an East African night in the wild was a testament to the awesome power of suggestibility over the human mind, especially from things that are unknown and unseen.

This is such an important subject, that I've decided to devote an entire chapter to it later in the book. As an afterthought here, I should mention that I slept soundly and peacefully for the remainder of my trip.

> *Most fears are based, not so much on current events or previous experience, but more on ignorance, inexperience or second-hand prejudices from authority figures or peers which render us incapable of separating reality from fantasy, and danger from opportunity.*

I quickly dressed in my Indiana Jones' outfit for our first safari drive, relieved that it would be conducted in full daylight, and strolled down the path to join my family for breakfast. Calvin Cottar, who was leading a walking safari that day, asked me if I had rested well. Smiling sheepishly, but with an exaggerated air of confidence, I replied, with a contrived answer I had heard my friend and fellow keynote speaker, Coach Lou Holtz, offer his audiences many times, "Great night. Very rejuvenating. I slept like a newborn baby. Woke up every half-hour and cried!"

We all laughed and admitted that it had been a long night for us dude-ranchers. One of my sons-in-law, Ladd, mentioned that he could see my shadow on the side of my tent through the trees, because my lantern—which he observed was going on and off intermittently—acted like a projector. He expressed concern that I might, unwittingly, have been using myself as lion bait and putting myself at risk. My other son-in-law, Tom, admitted that he had a sleep-deprived night like the rest of us, conjuring up several unsettling scenarios. This was music to my ears that my daughters' husbands, Tom Arnold and Dr. Ladd MacNamara, Tom a very successful investment banker in New York and Ladd a highly-qualified physician in Atlanta, shared my premonitions in the darkness

Calvin reassured us that it had been especially windy last night and that the wind was expected to be light for the remainder of our visit. He said the lions usually stay clear of the Maasai warriors and the camp, and that the ones we heard were probably several hundred yards or even a mile away. He smiled and told us that, if we were lucky, we might see a lioness who was nursing a new cub just above us on the side of the hill. Her routine was to hunt during the night and return just before sunrise. I glanced at my watch and swallowed, thinking that I may prefer observing her from the Land Rover or Jeep, rather than meet her on the path on my way to breakfast; my breakfast not hers!

Commenting also that there was a male leopard living nearby who enjoyed snoozing by the dining tent on occasion, Calvin introduced us to our personal guide and spotter, and strolled away to meet his party for a hike through the bush. He referred to the leopard as if it was a welcome house guest. I, on the other hand, had been unnerved by the wind. Putting our apprehensions from the previous night behind, we could hardly wait to take our first game drive.

Sporting a grin as big as a grand piano, standing straight and tall as a Kenyan marathoner, we met a very special man, destined to become like a brother to me and a friend for life to my family. Born and raised in Maasailand, John Sampeke offered us a wealth and knowledge of animals, birds, insects, flora, fauna and an intimate overview of Maasai culture and traditions, impossible to gain from any other one person. John passed the Kenya professional Safari Guides' Association examinations with the top grades in his class.

Highly educated, quietly entertaining with a Bob Newhart sense of humor, John is unquestionably the best Maasai professional guide in the business, having nearly fifteen years' experience working with the most reputable safari companies in Kenya. During breakfast and later, throughout our weeklong adventure by his side, John gave us wildlife, botany and history lessons that no amount of money or material possessions can replace. He made learning fun and exciting.

Chapter Five
The Maasai: Back to the Future

Our initial exploration drive was via the classic Rolls, which Debi

had christened "Chitty-chitty-bang-bang" from an old Dick Van Dyke

movie. It certainly didn't have the suspension or feel of a Lexus sedan,

but was sturdy as a tank, accommodated the whole family, had good

viewing visibility and, after all, was the way you traveled first class back

in the 1920s. John introduced us to Sambe, our spotter who rode on top

of the vehicle to search for wildlife in the distance.

As we headed downhill from Cottars' camp out onto the grasslands of

the Mara, we came across a herd of about forty cattle tended by an ado-

lescent Maasai boy. John mentioned that boys at this age spend virtually

all their time looking after cattle, having been brought up to regard them

not merely as wealth, but as an extension of themselves. The Maasai

herder must know everything about each animal, and keep track of all

of them at all times, seldom sitting down to avoid the embarrassment

and shame of losing one. This learning process includes identifying the

tracks, sounds and habits of predators such as lions, hyenas and leopards.

> "May God give you children, and may God give you cattle" John recited. In Maasai prayers these are always together, because having children the family will need cattle to sustain them; and if they have cattle, they will want children to herd and care for them

Of course children are more important than cattle, which we witnessed spending time in one of their villages. And although cattle are the symbols of status and success, the Maasai believe that a family with many children and no cattle is far richer than one with no children and many cattle.

Before meeting John, our guide—who is a highly-regarded junior elder in his Maasai clan—my impressions of his culture had been typical of most westerners.

> To us outsiders, the Maasai fit our romantic image of what African tribal people should be. Attired in toga-like red robes, adorned with ocher and beaded jewelry, carrying swords, long spears or staffs, they are indelible in a timeless African dream. And, in truth, they have stubbornly attempted to keep their heritage intact and remain visibly confident in their identity as a people.

The origins of the Maasai are shrouded in mystery and legend. The word Maasai, according to John, literally means "one who speaks the language *Maa*." Their roots are considered to have stemmed from the Nilotes, of the Nile region, and the Cushites of North Africa. Observing the Maasai attire, there are hints of ancient Romans from North Africa. The Maasai sword resembles the short Roman fighting sword; the warriors' hairstyle is shaped like a Roman helmet; and the toga and sandals seem to be styled similar to those of Romans.[i]

And like the ancient Romans, the Maasai were experts at war, intimidating their enemies with the same overwhelming attack style employed by the famed Roman legions. Imagine their frightening advance in a sea of red paint, Colobus monkey anklets, tall headdresses fashioned from black ostrich feathers and lions' manes. Armed with spears, swords and buffalo-hide shields, they chased their rivals out of their villages.

Perhaps one socially redeeming aspect of the Maasai reputation for fierceness and aggression is that until a little over a century ago the slave traders, settlers and agriculturists were hindered by their respect and/or fear of the Maasai, and, as a result, the interior of East Africa remained relatively untouched.

They are an athletic coach's dream team, especially those Maasai warriors we observed, all with a vertical jump of over three feet, ideally suited to win the slam-dunk competition in the National Basketball

> *I have never seen more impressive physical attributes inherent in one group of people. Tall, lean, strong, self-assured, with chiseled facial features and large, penetrating eyes, not a single Maasai man or woman we encountered had need for a "low-carb" diet or liposuction.*

Association back home. They may not be able to out-run a lion in terms of speed, but they can outlast a lion when it comes to distance and endurance. They also are completely fearless and I observed that trait in John Sampeke, who had killed a large lion when he was a young Maasai warrior, armed only with a spear.

John told us that his ancestors believed that Engai (God) had ordained that they should own all the earth's cattle and that their raids, therefore, were simply an exercise in recovering misplaced property. As selfish a motive as this appears for a culture to maintain, the Maasai have been unjustly exploited since colonial times, as the Europeans and British confiscated and claimed much of the Maasai land taking advantage of their naivety concerning titles, borders, boundaries and fences.

Listening to John, I could not help but reflect on many of the keynote speeches I have given to corporate and public audiences throughout the world concerning the misguided notion of success being a status you purchase or arrive at, rather than a process you experience.

> To the Maasai, land is God's property not man's property. As a pastoral people, moving with their herds as nomads, the Maasai saw themselves as caretakers, reasoning that since wildlife had always been free to migrate from millennia to millennia, why shouldn't they? They considered cattle as their gifts from God, but they considered land as theirs to use, but never to own.

Ownership is not the measure of achievement. Employment, utilization, and conservation are. While I do not condone the taking of someone else's property, be it a cow, money or land, I do fervently believe that humans don't really own anything, no matter how desperately they try to build monuments to their progress, pyramids to house their treasures and mummies, real estate, gold bullion, jewelry to dazzle their adoring fans and estate planners to parcel out their spoils to their heirs.

As a capitalist and free enterpriser, with a win-win, stewardship mentality, I consider each of us individuals, in this digital, instant-access, modern world, to be likened to a cattle herder, gardener, house sitter, yacht tender, caretaker or land squatter for but a moment in time. To presume otherwise is to miss the whole point of being alive and connected to the natural world, past, present and future. Sometimes in the most humbling and humble surroundings, the stark truth hits you right between the eyes.

> *One of my soul-deep encounters with wisdom, is the revelation that its not what you have that counts, it is what you are continuing to do with what you have.*

The Maasai dwellings we saw were low igloo-shaped huts, constructed of woven branches and stuffed with leaves, appearing like inverted baskets, smeared with cow dung as their exterior finish to provide shelter from the wind and rain. As we drove toward them, they seemed like giant, smooth termite mounds, blending naturally into the surrounding terrain.

We entered the village or *enkang* through an opening in the thick wall of dried thorn-tree branches around the circle of houses, which protected the enclave from lions, leopards and hyenas. Each married woman has the responsibility to build her family's home and John asked one of them for permission to look inside her residence.

We had to bend down to enter the narrow opening into the interior which consisted of one room. It had one sleeping area large enough for several people to sleep together, and a smaller one more privately located for the mother of the house and her young children. Sitting on the larger bed, while our eyes adjusted to the darkness, we observed that it was made from strong tree branches covered with soft, stretched hides.

The woman was stirring curdled milk from a gourd and mixing it with meal. Their main food staples appeared to be milk, a type of yogurt, meat and blood from their livestock, and honey. The hearth was placed in the center of the house, used for cooking, warmth and light. The only other opening was in the ceiling, directly above the hearth to let the light in and the smoke from the fire out.

Along the side of one interior wall there was a manger-like den, with a barrier separating it from the rest of the house, for goat kids and infant calves. They were quite friendly and noisy and we conjectured that they would be very reliable "alarm clocks" every morning at sunrise.

Strong arguments can be made about certain rituals and practices that favor a paternalistic society in which women are subservient. But as the Scriptures wisely counsel us, "Let him without sin cast the first stone." It is nonsense for anyone in our western culture, steeped in violence, hedonism and class struggles, to pass judgment on another culture and scold them for their lifestyles.

> I, and my family, preferred to look for the good in how the Maasai live, rather than behave like some kind of cultural missionaries.

Unquestionably, the rank and privilege in Maasai society favor the males, who progress through a kind of scout-troop merit badge hierarchy based upon time in rank and certain ritualistic achievements. Every Maasai male is assigned to a group based upon age, a system giving him a sense of belonging, consisting of three life stages—childhood, warriorhood and elderhood.

At the bottom of the hierarchy are the children, or *inkera.* Before adolescence, males and females, do minor chores, including herding young animals like the ones we had seen inside the dwelling.

We were struck by the laughter and mischievous playfulness of all the young children. There was no whining or fussing and they addressed all the adults as "Father" or "Mother." Watching them romping, giggling, playing hide and seek, and stick and ball games, I thought back to my television-less childhood.

> What had we done before TV? Played outdoors, used our imaginations and exercised. It begs the question about progress. Is a couch-potato better off and more advanced than a child on the Mara?

The next age group consists of boys between 14 and 18 who have been circumcised. Prior to circumcision, a ceremony called *Alamal*

Lengipaata is held, during which the boys receive a new generational name, moving on from *inkera*. Circumcision, or *emorata*, signifies the transition from youth to manhood and the boy is expected to remain stoic and show no sign of pain during the process. After the ritual, he becomes a junior warrior, expected to be a role model who is strong, gentle, clever, wise and courageous and who can enjoy both hunting and poetry. The junior warriors, or *ilmoran*, reside in their own settlements called *emanyata*, with their mothers and younger siblings, and are charged with protecting their community, livestock and grazing areas from intruders.

The junior warriors then move up to senior warriors, having met certain physical, age and cultural requirements. The next rank advancement is to junior elder, when, in addition to settling down in marriage and family responsibilities, they decide important questions affecting the community, and also are granted the power to bless and to curse.

I asked John, who, at the time was a junior elder almost ready to progress to senior elderhood, what the power to conjure up a curse or *ol-deket* granted him. Giving me that incredible, natural "toothpaste commercial" smile of his, he said that such a curse will bring havoc and dire consequences to the unfortunate recipient, but only if the cursed victim deserves the punishment.

I vowed never to make him angry with me and promised to be a model safari client. Judging from his countenance and laid-back adapt-

47

ability to meet any unforeseen surprise, I doubted that John had ever or would ever exercise his power to cast a negative spell on anyone. But, for "curse" insurance, I sat up front next to him on every game drive, flattered him continually, and followed his instructions to the letter.

And, if you believe that, I'd like to sell you the first snowmobile franchise in Kenya! I sat up front so I could see everything he saw, praised his encyclopedic knowledge because it was so interesting and informative, and followed his instructions because he was the guide and I was a two-legged, out-of-shape novice high on the food chain.

The ultimate goal for the Maasai man is the move up to senior elderhood, which John said he was looking forward to. Senior elders include medicine men, spiritual leaders and judges, all of whom are expected to be wise, disciplined, patient and conscientious. Their main activities include settling disputes, teaching and passing on lore from the past, and reflecting on life. Of course, a learned and skilled man like John, has one foot firmly planted on the Mara as Kenya's premier Maasai safari guide and the other foot planted solidly with his own family life near Nairobi.

My two daughters were very interested in the roles of the young Maasai girls and women which did not follow the same structured career path as the males, nor offer the same liberties. Admittedly, we were in the remote outback of East Africa far away from city life, where Maasai women, as well as men, are asserting themselves more in every

> *John Sampeke is unique in that he is comfortable in both the modern world and in the savage paradise, and can make the transition from one to the other as if he were simply changing clothes instead of stepping into a time machine. He can handle a laptop or a lion with equal deftness and looks at home in khakis, a business suit or his red toga, although it is easy to discern at a glance which he would prefer if he had only one choice.*

professional field as formal education, skill development and knowledge provide them with awareness for opportunities that never existed for them before.

However, I could sense my girls' discomfort with some of the disparities between male and female lifestyles, including the fact that the men could have more than one wife, and that each wife had to build her own home out of branches, leaves and cow dung. The good news is that they are devoted mothers, talented clothing and jewelry designers, hard workers who seem happy and at peace, and who can build their homes, literally, any darned way they want to. They decide how big they want them, design them, and then do the construction themselves.

In recognition of women's position in the *enkang*, houses are considered to be their private property. Although men are heads of families, women are heads of houses, and a husband is not allowed to enter the house without his wife's permission, which elicited a high-five exchange between Debi and Dayna as a token consolation. Also, we were told about the practice—which may or may not be totally enforced today—which allows the other women in the village to beat a man who mistreats his wife, seize his cattle and abandon him to take care of the children and himself. We thought this could certainly discourage the kind of spousal abuse we have been sweeping under the carpet in our own country.

> Marriage, in Maasailand, is not simply a bond and exchange of vows between individuals, but also between families.

A mistreated wife often returns to her family and if there is evidence that the husband was cruel, the marriage is dissolved. However, divorce is uncommon among the rural Maasai, because a council of elders is there—for a couple experiencing domestic difficulties—to listen, to discuss the issues involved and to encourage the couple to resolve their differences. In America, easy come, easy go. Just head to Vegas for one or the other in a drive-through.

I could devote an entire book to the traditions, ceremonies, lifestyles and challenges of these amazing people, the true landlords of this area we were privileged to be visiting.

All we really wanted to achieve in spending a few hours in one village was to see the children at play, observe their cheerfulness and innocence, and carry with us a morsel of empathy and understanding of what daily life was like for these "real" Maasai on the Mara in the twenty-first century.

We were there in the present tense, glimpsing at the past.

It is clear that the Maasai are on a collision course with the future. Their customs survive and endure, but their society, as such, may not. They are an endangered species as surely as the rhino and tiger are in their bulldozed habitats. Change is inevitable and not always for the better.

The authority of traditional Maasai elders has diminished significantly as the government has appointed or influenced the election of leaders and representatives beyond the local community. The reduction of grazing land due to agricultural and housing expansion is restricting their movements, much like a rapidly drying, overpopulated water hole does to its inhabitants during a drought. The old system of bartering livestock for labor is no longer common. Food selection is based more on survival than choice. The gap between the rich and poor is widening. Infant mortality and illiteracy rates are high. Water is scarce. All these factors are forcing the tough realities of urbanization or extinction, of going modern or going nowhere.

Back in our vehicle, we headed out of the *enkang* waving at the children until we could no longer see them. Forever the optimist, I still felt the Maasai would be in the Mara as long as there are the endless migrations of the great herds; as long as there are lions in the tall grass; and as long as there are wildlife conservationists like Calvin and Louise Cottar and educated elders like John Sampeke. Sometimes a few individuals can reroute a torrential river and change destiny.

> One thing is certain about the people of the Maasai Mara. They are resilient and proud. They have a saying that has been handed down through the centuries that serves them well. Erisyo laikin o kaa. "Defeat and death are the same thing." They will never surrender. You can't keep a Maasai caged like an animal in the zoo. They were born free and I pray they will find the ingenuity, resources and guidance to endure.

Their fate is inexorably woven into that of our own society. No society has ever survived its own success, nor has any empire. Pass in review: Ming Dynasty, Maya, Inca, Aztec, Egypt, The Roman Empire, Sparta, the Vikings, The French Empire, the British Empire or the Soviet Union to name a few. The hackneyed adage holds true: "Unless we learn from history, we are bound to repeat it." Is the American empire the next lesson in indulgence, hubris, resource squandering and shortsightedness? Can the wildlife and peoples of East Africa offer us any wise counsel? They've certainly been there and done that, so the cliché goes.

What lessons were there this morning for my daughters, sons-in-law and me? We discussed these as we headed out to explore the unknown. I jotted a little list in my diary dated August 21st:

I closed the diary and picked up my binoculars. We were outside and ready to play.

We wondered who was tracking us while we thought we were tracking them.

> • Simplify our lives. Stop collecting. Start celebrating, for no apparent reason.
> • Gather memories instead of memorabilia.
> • Do some genealogy about our family ancestors. What were their lives like? What soul-deep legacy, if any, did they pass on to us? What did we learn and love most about our parents and grandparents?

- What will we gladly give up to improve the quality of our lives?
- What will we never give up, no matter what?
- Dream as if we had forever. Live as if this was the only day.
- Don't just treat everyone the way we want to be treated. Treat everyone the way they should be treated to believe they can reach their full potential, based upon their own beliefs and heritage
- Never judge a person by her cow-dung house. She may be healthier, happier and wiser than us, and probably is
- It's not nice to fool with Mother Nature
- Love what you have, even if you don't have all that you'd love
- We are all different, on a safari heading in the same direction

CHAPTER SIX
THE GREAT MIGRATION

It's one thing to look down from a plane and see the herds of wildebeest, along with their traveling companions zebra and antelope, move from the Serengeti to the Mara, and an entirely different scenario to be at the epicenter of this earth-trembling event. Television documentaries, videos and photos simply can't do it justice. These inadequate word pictures I am serving up to you certainly will not.

> *You need to be there at ground zero to witness one of the remaining wonders of the world.*

The Maasai Mara Game Reserve in Kenya runs down to the Tanzania border, where it continues as the great Serengeti Plain with its famed national park. Adding the Mara's 320 square kilometers to this, you have a continuous wildlife reserve almost the size of New England in the United States. The official designation of the Maasai Mara is as a park reserve, which differs from a national park in that a park reserve allows inhabitants to graze their animals and shoot game if they are attacked.

National parks set aside the entire area for wildlife and the natural environment, with no allowances for pastoral grazing.

The Serengeti in Tanzania is at its best for wildlife safaris during December through May, a period of intermittent rains. At that time huge herds of wildebeests and zebras are centered in the open plains in the southern part of the region. The Mara is at is best in July and August, when the migration from the Serengeti is in full force.

The Maasai Mara lies in the Great Rift Valley, which is a fault line some 3,500 miles long, stretching from Ethiopia's Red Sea through Kenya, Tanzania, Malawi and into Mozambique. There are four major types of topography in the Mara: Ngama Hills to the east with sandy soil and leafy bushes which are a favorite food of the rare black rhino; the Oloololo Escarpment forming the western boundary and rising to a magnificent plateau; the Mara Triangle bordering the Mara River with lush grassland and acacia woodlands supporting masses of game, especially migrating wildebeest; and the Central Plains forming the largest part of the reserve, with scattered bushes and boulders on rolling grasslands favored by the plains game.

The estimates vary widely, by as much as a half-million, but there are said to be over a million and a half wildebeests or gnu in the region, and their numbers are increasing. Even on our first outing, we felt as if we had seen them all, although we had only seen a few thousand. Lions, hyenas, cheetahs, wild dogs and leopards try to maintain the balance, but prey has outstripped the predators in their case.

Looking at their neverending marching armies through binoculars from our Land Rover, they still appeared in the distance—as they had from the air—as great hoards of ants speckling the plain.

Up close they are a fascinating hybrid. Pewter colored, white-bearded creatures whose heads appear too large for their bodies, they can be likened to a stunted, anorexic version of our American bison or, reversing the analogy, our American bison look like obese, fast-food-gorged wildebeests on steroids.

In the midst of the thundering masses, we caught a glimpse of what our own native Americans must have experienced hundreds of years ago when over 30 million bison roamed the plains of the United States and Canada.

Wildebeests are noisy. They emit a harsh grunt that sounds like a large male ram and an old man with a frog in his throat. Many people find them ugly or ungainly, but we thought them handsome in their own comedic way, although we named them all "Joe," because they all looked the same to us, with the exception of the young wildebeests whose horns are straight, and not yet curved.

With large heads, high shoulders, sloping hind quarters and thin, spindly legs, they appear uncoordinated until you watch them cavort and gallop. They are surprisingly agile and can achieve full speed rapidly and zigzag constantly when frightened, which is their only defense from predators.

The wildebeest actual means of survival is in their sheer numbers. As if nature had whispered a secret to them, they time the birthing of their calves within about thirty days of each other, all in the month of February.

The mother wildebeest, who gives birth lying down, immediately gets up, thus breaking the umbilical cord. The baby is on its feet and running with its mother and the rest of the herd within six or seven minutes of its birth, which may be a record for four-legged mammalian coordination. All calves are light brown with black faces and have no distinguishing features from one another. The calves recognize their mothers by the sound of their grunts, while the mothers recognize their calves by their smell. As hard as I tried, I could not tell the difference in any sounds made by the thousands of wildebeests we saw and heard, and was puzzled to consider that a million and a half of them could recognize each others voices and greetings. Go figure!

Considering that the area provides the food requirements for an incalculable number of wildebeests, zebras, topis and gazelles, as well as giraffes, black rhinoceroses, buffaloes, elands and over twenty species of other antelopes, we asked John, our guide, how the grasslands could support this profusion of large herbivores without being exhausted. John explained that almost all the species are separated ecologically, some by their food requirements and some by their preferences for different types of grassland—open or wooded, dry or swampy. It is a kind of synergy by natural design. Waterbuck and reedbuck are located mainly in swampy grassland, and feed primarily on grass. Impala and Grant's gazelles nibble the leaves of bushes, in addition to eating grass, so they are found in wooded grassland or bush.

Wildebeests, zebras, topis and Thomson's gazelles are grazers, so they inhabit mostly the open plains. Although these four species may feed from the same grass plants, they do not compete because their eating takes place at different stages of the plants' growth. Initially, the zebras eat the outer part of the stem which is too tough for the antelope. Zebras have incisors in both jaws to cut through wiry stems and their digestive systems can better deal with this less nutritious type of food.

Next come the topis, whose pointed muzzles enable them to get to the lower parts of the stems. With square muzzles, the wildebeests dine on the horizontal leaves and a few days after this efficient mowing and trimming by the larger grazers, new grass sprouts from the base and provides food for the diminutive Thomson gazelles.

Even the huge Cape buffaloes do their part in maintaining a healthy pasture. Feeding mainly at night, they nuzzle beneath the tougher top growth of the grass and eat the sweeter green shoots underneath. In the process, they trample some of the tough, uneaten stems which become mulch to stimulate new plant growth.

And so this continuous cycle repeats itself through the millennia. After a half-year of grazing in Tanzania's Serengeti, the promise of rain and fresh life-giving grass beckons more than a million wildebeests together in July and August into a single massive herd pouring across the border north into the Mara.

The mile-high Mara region receives good rains. Thunderstorms from Lake Victoria, sixty miles to the west, refresh its plains over an extended wet season. The rains nurture a fifty-mile-wide expanse of rich savanna, framed between the Loita Hills and the steep Oloololo (or Siria) Escarpment, which abruptly marks the Mara's western district. Primarily open country, the Mara's tree-flecked grasslands are broken by occasional hillocks and patches of thicker brush.

During and after the rains, the Mara flushes radiant green. In the dry months, the muted greens of brush and the dark ribbons of gallery forest are counterpoints to plains of golden grass. In every season the Mara is a magic land of wide vistas, alive with every type of wildlife, including over fifty species of birds of prey.

Like an alien invasion from a Lord of the Rings movie sequel, the migrating herds of wildebeests create an aura of swirling dust and a sea of hooves as they make their spectacular entrance in a surging column of soldiers stretching from horizon to horizon.

At the Mara River, we sat spellbound as the wildebeests massed together on the banks as if waiting for a whistle from the referee before plunging forward into the treacherous waters to get to the other side. But this was not a sporting event. It was the game of life being replayed through the centuries. An armada of crocodiles, some more than fifteen feet long, silently took position in their path like submarines waiting for helpless cargo ships. I could feel myself quietly cheering for the wildebeest and zebras to make safe passage through the swift, murky currents and past the deadly prehistoric jaws.

The throngs that survive the raging waters and countless predators graze on the lush grass of the Mara before making the six-hundred-mile return trip south to the Serengeti in October before the rainy season. Once back in Tanzania, the young wildebeest calves are birthed in February, giving them time to grow sufficiently strong to undertake the long march north six months later.

> I didn't say much on our way back to camp. The entire experience was so overwhelming that it takes an inordinate amount of mental and emotional processing. In a word it is humbling.

A safari is a crash course in separating the significant from the insignificant. The world's most awesome natural outdoor spectacle of the Great Migration is unimaginable. It made me, who had considered myself at the center of the universe, feel like an oboe player in a grand orchestra consisting of one Maestro and billions of musicians in a never-ending symphony. I had my part but I was not a soloist or virtuoso, and my contribution to the outcome so brief that the notes I played would scarcely seem like the blink of an eye in the overall scheme of things.

Too often, because of our reasoning abilities and therefore our rationalization for our weaknesses and justification for our unwarranted belief in our superiority over all other life forms, we are disconnected from the natural world as if we are a sophisticated audience enjoying the performance, separated from the players by the orchestra pit.

There on the Mara, I was reconnected with the orchestra and the symphony. It was clear that there is no audience, no orchestra pit. We all are part of the same unfinished music, part of the balance of nature. If we try to sit on the outside, it is we who are out of balance and sync.

> I wrote in my diary these three words:
>
> Timelessness. Humility. Harmony.

CHAPTER SEVEN
STRIPPING AWAY THE MASKS

Arriving back at camp a bit weary and numb from the action, we showered, changed clothes and joined the other guests around the campfire. Among the many pleasant surprises that greeted us were the crisp, cool evenings that invited a light sweatshirt and a glass of red wine or sherry by the fire. As I mentioned earlier, both the altitude and dryness of our site discouraged the presence of mosquitoes—helping make this nightly ritual around the fire one of the most memorable aspects of our trip.

All of the delicious food and beverages, including the appetizers and fine wine around the campfire, were included at no extra charge. By the end of my second safari the following year, I was so laid back and at home with the environment and the guides and other resident staff at the Cottars 1920s camp that we all felt like brothers and sisters at an annual family reunion. Calvin and Louise are very generous with some of the finest wines I have ever sampled, but I think they were not expecting to return from a supply trip to Nairobi to find that the guides and I had finished off about eight bottles of their best reserves from the liquor cabinet, while getting carried away with recounting our most exaggerated "close calls" and wildlife adventure stories until the wee hours of the morning.

There is no question that I enjoyed enough food and drink to make my presence a non-profit event for the Cottars, but they know plenty about human interaction and behavior, along with their knowledge of animal and wildlife behavior and provided an atmosphere that fostered a total transformation from the personas we thought we were back home to who we really were without our self-styled masks of pretenders.

My family and I have discussed this vulnerability many times as we have reflected on the lessons learned and perspective gained from our safaris. Each guest was simply a new friend dressed in khakis, having a chat around a fire. We discussed the stars and constellations which shone brighter than any of us could ever remember, even those of us who had seen the stars from a mountain top, desert or in the middle of the ocean without the presence of clouds, haze or the ozone layer.

> The most interesting aspect of these evening rendez-vous around the fire was that no one ever talked about business, personal problems or the upheavals in the world at large. In that setting, it was impossible to think of these issues. We only spoke of beauty, grandeur, childlike excitement and discovery

In all of my trips there, only once did I observe a non-participant, a business executive, chain-smoking with his satellite cell phone glued to his ear, doing deals and giving orders to his stressed-out staff in his office seven thousand miles away. He only stayed a day or so and moved on with an itinerary that looked as long as floor-to-ceiling Venetian blinds, strung together as if the object was some kind of "race around the world" reality show or scavenger hunt to see how many items on the list could be checked off within a week.

Not once around the Cottars' campfire did any of us speak about our careers, our material possessions, our achievements or our positions back home. What good was all that out here anyway? What use was it, for that matter, to try to impress each other so that the others would think we were uniquely important or accomplished?

Nor did we ever discuss political or religious beliefs. Here in the Maasai Mara, orthodoxy, dogma and all those rules over which the different sects fight each other seemed more irrelevant than ever.

One by one, the disguises and trappings of our status-oriented civilization and the images with which we adorned ourselves and projected to others were being stripped away. Every evening, staring into the dancing flames that twisted and turned with each shift in the East African wind, I felt more naked and transparent.

> *Did God really intend for us to argue and kill each other over whose view of Creation was most authentic? In Africa, it is more basic. God is everywhere, leading the migrating herds, in the star-studded sky overhead, in the earth at our feet and in the air we were breathing. Most of all, God's presence could be felt within our very souls as ubiquitous, constant and eternal.*

As I let go, I sensed the futility in all my posturing to be noticed as special, a winner and somehow better than the herds of wildebeests or masses of humanity throughout the world. The relief was indescribable.

> *It was like shedding an outer skin or veneer that hid the child inside; the ever-curious, searching boy-man who I really was.*

After my family and all the other guests had retired for the evening, I stayed for a while as the coals turned a deep glowing reddish-amber among the rocks and ashes. My Maasai warrior guide stood patiently with a lantern in his hand and his spear by his side waiting to escort me up the dark, winding path to my tent.

I thought back to my first major literary effort, *Seeds of Greatness*, written twenty years earlier and found myself reciting a passage of prose I had offered in the first chapter, reminding the reader that these words could have been written by some inner voice that hides, unseen, in each of us, gently sighing of our fragile sensitivity and preoccupation with our own self-consciousness:

"Don't be fooled by me. Don't be fooled by the face I wear. I wear a mask. I wear a thousand masks—masks that I'm afraid to take off; and none of them is me.

Pretending is an art that is second nature to me, but don't be fooled. I give the impression that I am secure, that all is sunny and unruffled within me as well as without; that confidence is my name and coolness my game, that the water is calm and I am in command; and that I need no one. But don't believe me, please. My surface may seem smooth, but my surface is my mask, my ever-varying and ever-concealing mask.

Beneath lies no smugness, no complacence. Beneath dwells the real me in confusion and aloneness. But I hide that. I don't want anybody to know it. I panic at the thought of my weakness being exposed.

That's why I frantically create a mask to hide behind—a nonchalant, sophisticated façade—to help me pretend, to shield me from the glance that knows. But such a glance is precisely my salvation, my only salvation, and I know it. That is, if it's followed by acceptance; if it's followed by love.

It's the only thing that can liberate me from myself, from my own self-built prison wall, from the barriers I so painstakingly erect. It's the only thing that will assure me of what I can't assure myself—that I am really something.

Who am I, you may wonder. I am someone you know very well. I am every man you meet. I am every woman you meet. I am every child you meet. I am right in front of you. Please...love me.[ii]

As I got up from the canvas director's chair, inspecting the fire pit to ensure that no embers could blow inadvertently into the dry grass nearby, I took a deep breath and exhaled slowly, relishing how exhilarating and freeing this trip was for me. I was a man who loved life and adored his family. I was trying to live my years without conceit or a trace of arrogance, striving to plant shade trees for future generations who I would never meet in person. I was hoping to live a life of significance by accepting my own insignificance in the big picture, while appreciating the miracle and privilege of the gift of life for its own sake, not for something I needed to prove. I thought of all the mistakes I had made throughout my life, as a son, student, military officer, husband, business professional, father and friend.

> I then imagined crushing all my faults together in a ball, like a giant wad of scrap paper, and flinging it into the fire pit, watching it burst into flames and disappear into a wisp of smoke, carrying with it all the guilt trips and remorse I had toted like stone weights for the previous wrongs that I could never make right.

I decided on that August night to let go of my fear of rejection and feelings of inadequacy and embrace the concepts of unconditional love and acceptance. I vowed to forgive those who had hurt me and to forgive myself for all the inadvertent hurts I had caused. A Kenya mountainside is the ideal setting for such lofty aims.

When I think of self-love, I don't see it as narcissism or selfish worship of the man or woman in the mirror. I believe self-esteem is a healthy ability to share—with others—the value you feel inside yourself, without

> *Many times since, people have asked me what the most important thing you should take with you on a tented safari in East Africa. I always answer, "If you don't love yourself, and life, you will be lost, ill at ease or bored."*

expecting a quid pro quo payoff. When I consider the word "soul" as I'm referring to it in this book, I believe it is the purity and beauty of an individual's core values. Core values radiate like rings, as when a leaf falls in a pond.

The self-centered individuals, who to me are desperately looking for meaning in all the wrong places and in all the wrong faces, constantly seek approval from and power over others. They try to impress them with their worth rather than express concern for others' well-being. And their outward appearances, or masks, usually involve ways to hide their real thoughts and intentions.

> *A personal proverb I use to remind me of my true core values is that: "I feel worthy of the best but not more worthy than the rest."*

In other words, I see the Maasai, the lions, the wildebeests, birds, butterflies, fish and trees as having an equal right to life and the opportunity to reach their full potential as I do, and I appreciate my own role in enriching my own self-actualization and theirs in a symbiotic team effort.

The value-centered people I know give of themselves freely and graciously, constantly seeking to empower others. If I've accomplished nothing else of significance in my life, I have tried to instill that character trait in each of my children, and am subtly demonstrating that virtue by example for my grandchildren. Open, modest and value-centered individuals have no need or room for conceit, which I feel is the opposite of core value.

Feeling good about who they are, and not needing to gush about their victories or line their walls with celebrity milestones, people with core values spend much of their time "paying value" as I call it, to others. When praised, they say "thank you" and share the spotlight. When they make mistakes, they view them as learning experiences and accept responsibility.

My friend Nathaniel Branden has taught me and countless others that self-esteem can't be bought, won in an arena, measured by a stock portfolio or trophy heads of the "Big Five" game animals on the wall of your den. Self-esteem is a soul-deep belief that you deserve to be happy and successful, combined with a trust or confidence in an ability to manage life's challenges as they present themselves. It is as necessary for human development as oxygen, as basic as the carbon from which diamonds are formed. I used to think that diamonds were so sought after because they glitter, but discovered that their value is in their rarity and ability to endure. Formed at the earth's core, they hold their value indefinitely.

> *Perhaps you already have developed the wisdom to know that the diamonds you seek are waiting to be discovered in your own back yard—the back yard of your mind and in your heart of hearts—where you need to dig deeply at your very center where your sense of values and your self-worth are embedded.*

I now consider East Africa, and in particular, this enchanting camp in the Kenya highlands of the Maasai Mara to be my own back yard. It is my second home, just as it may have been ancient man's first home, and the original Eden. I am at my best when I am here, because there is so much to witness, to explore, to embrace and to love.

There are many definitions and interpretations of love. I've always looked at love as unconditional acceptance and "looking for the good." Perhaps one of the best and most appropriate descriptions of love is that given by Dr. Gerald Jampolsky, a well-known psychiatrist, author and founder of the Center for Attitudinal Healing in Tiburon, California. Dr.

Jampolsky has devoted decades of his life teaching children and adults who are experiencing emotional and physical crises that "love is letting go of fear."

With love, there is no room or reason for fear. Love is natural and unconditional. Love asks no questions—neither preaching nor demanding; neither comparing nor measuring.

> Love is—purely and simply—the greatest value of all. And, most importantly, we must feel love inside ourselves before we can give it to others.

Fundamental, isn't it? If there is no deep, internal value inside us, then we have nothing of inner value to give to or share with others. Putting on one of our many masks to hide the lightly valued self within, we can act as if we need other people, we can be dependent upon them, we can look for security in them or approval from them we can indulge them, flatter them, and attempt to purchase their affection. But we cannot share or give an emotion to anyone else, unless we first have that emotion inside ourselves.

This concern about holding onto or possessing love, as if it were a piece of artwork or jewelry, is how many relationships are perceived, pursued and destroyed. Authentic love makes you want to free yourself and those you love from the ties that bind and constrict. This is the kind

> Love is not fulfilling our expectations through someone else, nor possessing another person to make us whole. Love is giving and sharing and is the ultimate expression of synergy and the double win.

of feeling that permeates the air around the fire after witnessing the great migration of the herds.

This internal dialogue was getting a bit heady and heavy, so I walked silently beside the Maasai warrior to my tent. I wondered what he would think about my musings and ponderings, but knew he had no desire or use for such complexities. He smiled and bid goodnight in the "Maa" language. I looked directly into his eyes, nodded and returned his smile.

> He knew who he was, where he was, and why he was here in Maasailand. He had no need to wear a mask to appear to be someone else.

CHAPTER EIGHT
THE JUNGLE IS NEUTRAL

Early the next morning, at sunrise, we were off again on another game run. The ride was a little smoother since the "Chitty-chitty-bang-gang" Rolls was passed on to another party and our family was transported in one of the Cottars' fleet of nearly new Land Rovers. We asked John Sampeke what we were going to see that day.

His answer was as simple as it was profound. "We will see what we will see. What we don't see today, we may see tomorrow. Whatever wildlife desires to be seen, will reveal itself to us."

Tourists are a motley bunch, us included. Like unruly school children on a field trip, most of us get antsy unless there is non-stop action like MTV. I'm convinced that the entire industrialized world, especially the United States, is suffering from a special form of Attention Deficit Disorder (ADD) caused by sensory stimulation bombardment from electronic entertainment media and its resultant effect of immediate gratification need.

During the safaris I have gone on with my daughters and their husbands, and then with more of my children and grandchildren, we were fortunate to have a brilliant and patient Maasai guide in John Sampeke. He remarked in private that we were one of the most enjoyable groups he has ever guided because we were open to whatever happened and could sit quietly for long periods of time observing the wonders of birds, insects, lions and other wildlife without keeping score.

> To many tourists, a safari consists of shooting as many rolls of film as possible, keeping your eye fastened to your camcorder viewfinder and narrating your own home video to show the folks and friends back home that you were here and they weren't.

It is almost necessary to take two separate safaris: one to simply look, listen and learn; and another to make a photo or video documentary of your trip. When you're too busy taking photos, you often miss the nuances and, therefore, the real drama of what is transpiring all around you. It's like being the photographer at a wedding or a sports event. You may capture the proceedings, but you don't feel the emotion and you miss the important sidebars that are taking place, near and far.

We did take some great photos, which my daughters assembled in a captioned album as a Christmas present for me later that year. Both my sons-in-law wielded their camera equipment like *National Geographic* stringers on assignment, especially Dayna's husband, Tom, who had a set-up where the zoom lens alone cost more and had a better magnification range than my German infrared binoculars.

We had many marvelous encounters with elephant herds who enchanted us for hours on end. At the watering holes, the mothers had to scold and spank the baby elephants with their trunks to get them out of the natural pool after a forty-five minute drinkfest, mudfight, splashing contest and spray-the-adults-and-run game. The apparent family bonding, mutual affection and conscientiousness for the safety of their young was heartwarming.

Once, when we ventured too close, a large bull with impressive tusks came trumpeting out of the bush and began a charge toward our vehicle. Tom, who was sitting on the roof of the Land Rover, was clicking off some great action shots of the episode, but forgot to consider one important detail. He was viewing the scene through a super powerful zoom lens and, seeing the elephant charging us head-on, he tumbled back through the roof into the back seat to dodge the impending impact. The charge startled all of us, especially Tom, but our guide, John, laughed and said that all of us were more entertaining to him than the elephants. The bull elephant, John said, was only putting us on notice that we were irritating him and the others, with a mock charge. I looked at the giant bull elephant through Tom's zoom lens. Sure enough, he looked like his tusks would smash through the windshield at any moment and I found myself leaning back in my seat.

Just then the entire herd of about fifty elephants stampeded in all directions. Caught off guard again, we looked to John for reassurance. He said that they had seen a cobra in their midst, which is about the only living thing that would cause them to panic that suddenly. Although prides of lion will attack elephants, especially if they can isolate a small one, elephants normally live their lives without fear of predators (except for human poachers with high-powered rifles), especially when their babies are herded in the middle of all the adults to provide a safety barrier when they are grazing or on the move.

> I know I will never visit a zoo or fenced animal compound again, and neither will my family. There is no similarity between animals in the wild and animals in cages or confined spaces. In the wild they are magnificent. In a zoo, they are paranoid and lethargic, stoically accepting their sentences of life imprisonment, with no possibility of parole.

Having said that, I must make a qualifying statement that—because of human encroachment and diminishing habitat—perhaps the only way future generations will ever see African wildlife other than via filmed documentaries will be in game parks and reserves. My own University of San Diego at California scientists have predicted that up to 50 percent of all species in East Africa parks will become extinct within the next three centuries.

That's why we were ecstatic and somber at the same time. We were seeing our connection with the past in the present, knowing that our great-grandchildren and their offspring may never have the same opportunity in the future. We relished every sighting and encounter.

We laughed at the warthogs and their little piglets on their knees digging and shoveling with their snouts for tender roots, ever watchful for predators who view them as gourmet appetizers. We even were entranced with the hyenas, whose appearance always reminded us of marauding bandits, with powerful jaws that can pulverize even the strongest bones into a meal, and whose cowardly appearance belies their reputation as ruthless, cunning and relentless hunters. Just as we had laughed at the warthogs or "warties," as we called them, so did the hyenas laugh at us as we passed by close enough to touch them. Turn about is fair play.

Many books have been written about lions, who live in more abundance in the Maasai Mara than anywhere else on earth. Lions are, without question, the most splendid of all the plains dwellers and it is impossible to grow weary of watching them. During my several safaris I have spent more time just sitting quietly, in a Jeep or Land Rover, no more than five or six feet away, observing lion behavior. No two lions seem the same, and they are as much icons of history as they are animals. Are they really animals, or supernatural beings?

We saw them in every possible situation. Sleeping, hunting, stalking, eating, grooming and roaring. We let a rope dangle out of the back of our Land Rover to entice the young cubs to play tug of war. John cautioned us not to play the game with the one or two-year-olds, lest they get rambunctious and yank us out of the vehicle as if that were the object of the contest.

We spent more than an hour observing the courtship of a male and female. She would approach him tentatively and abruptly run off for a while. Then she would intercept him from another direction and nip at his mane before retreating. This went on for a half-hour. She would advance and turn back, then she would stop, roll over and wriggle on her back as if she were trying to scratch an unreachable itch, a gesture I have seen our domestic house cats do so many times through the years. Finally, she would get his undivided attention and the waiting game would be over.

Being a family who respects the privacy of our neighbors and all living things, we didn't stay there and gawk at their mating. After all, the twenty-second coupling would be repeated nearly two hundred times during the next forty-eight hours and we saw no good reason to get a "birds and bees" anatomy seminar there in the wild. When we brought my grandchildren there the following year, we also avoided the graphic finale to the courtship ritual among lions, reasoning that there was a more meaningful and appropriate time and place for their enlightenment on this particular subject.

One of the most memorable experiences we had was spending an hour within a few feet of a regal male and female lion lying next to one another in the tall savanna grass. Even in repose the sight of the massive head of the male, shaggy maned and heavy with self-assurance, on a body rippling with muscles, with a half-opened mouth revealing fearsome lower canines and powerful jaws, the sight produced an unconscious shot of adrenaline in our systems. The lioness was no less impressive. Lean, sleek, with a shiny golden coat, she had the shoulders of a weight lifter who could bench press over 250 pounds, and was more alert than her companion. It was obvious who the primary hunter was.

Their hypnotic, amber eyes focused on us for a moment and then they dismissed our presence completely as being irrelevant as if we were a small group of irritating flies, bothersome yet innocuous. They were not the least bit interested and concerned with who or what we were. They ruled this domain and they knew it. The female lion's breathing changed.

Lowering her chest to the ground, she began to make rumbling, guttural sounds, as if she were trying to clear her throat. John said this was the beginning of periodic "territorial broadcasting" to let other lions know that they were here, and that this particular place belonged to this pair.

Just as John said it would, the big male—as if compelled by the female—seemed to have no other choice but to follow suit. Less than three feet from my open window of our vehicle, he raised his huge head toward us and emitted an ever increasing volume of roars so loud that they shook the other windows of the Land Rover, echoing for miles in the distance. Stronger and stronger came the roars. I could imagine a group of lions in the grandstands of a highly-partisan American sporting event getting caught up in the moment, chanting with progressively louder battlecries: "USA! USA! USA!" But that's not what this lion's message was. I conjured up my own interpretation of his earth-shattering warnings: "This is mine! Stay away! I am here! Stay away!"

Lions are unique among the big cats. Not only are they the strongest of the plains predators, their strength is compounded by the fact that they live in prides. We studied prides of various sizes, ranging from seven to nineteen members. The size of a pride seems to be determined by the amount of prey in the region, the kind of terrain, and the availability of water. An average pride consists of perhaps four or five lionesses with cubs of different ages, and two or three accompanying males.

> *I know you will think I am embellishing this story to make it sound more exciting, but as my children are my witnesses, the male lion was so close to me and the lung power of his roaring so powerful that it nearly blew my safari hat off my head. I quickly rolled my window up half way, remarking that it was because of the dust kicked up by the morning breeze that was blowing, and had nothing to do with my fear of staring into the open jaws of a four-hundred pound tyrant in a grouchy mood.*

It is a matriarchal community with the core group consisting of related females, many of whom remain in the same pride throughout their lives. It is not unusual for a lioness and her cubs to live apart from the main pride, but she will always be accepted and welcomed by her pride members and rarely will venture beyond her pride's territorial boundaries. These boundaries are established by the males who regularly "mark their territories" with paw scrapes in the earth, claw marks on trees, and sprays of urine mixed with excretions from scent glands at the base of their tails, that leave a distinct odor that warns intruders like a "no trespassing sign."

The adult males in the pride are often related to each other, but—for the most part—unrelated to the pride females. This occurs because at the age of about three years, the young males are ostracized from the pride in which they were born. John showed us several of these nomadic males, in particular one group of three called "The Bad Boys," who we tracked and observed for many hours.

They reminded us of college guys on spring break. They were ready for adventure, mischief and partying, but didn't have a clue of how to effectively get an easy meal, without their extended family members to support them. Everything they did was by trial and error. We watched them attempt to set a trap among a herd of zebras in the middle of the day, which they botched completely. John said that they would have to rely on finding a wildebeest with a broken leg, resulting from an inadvertent zigzag into a gopher hole or hitting a boulder on the dead run, until they sharpened up their skills.

Like our "Bad Boys," these wandering young lions form what might be classed as bachelor clubs who survive on their own until they are old enough and assertive enough to challenge the current dominant male for possession of a pride of their own. This exalted position of "king of the pride" may last only two or three years before another younger, stronger challenger comes along to take the heavyweight championship title and crown away from the reigning monarch.

Lions' hunting methods may be among the main reasons they band together. Leopards lead a solitary existence, depending upon stealth and surprise. Cheetahs rely on their blazing burst of speed to run down gazelles on the open plains. Although extremely agile for their size, lions—because they are larger and slower—are masters of ambush and group hunting, especially when several lionesses team up together. Group hunting also gives lions the advantage of seeking out much larger animals like adult zebra, eland or large buffalo in the area which can provide meat for the pride for a period of several days.

> Lions are classified and depicted as ferocious killers, but their natural affection exceeds that of most humans. Not only do they fondle their young continuously, adult females and males greet each other lovingly, caress and groom each other and lick one another regularly and often. The more we observed them, and the more John, our guide, informed us, the less frightened we became of the myths and jungle movies that had cast them as ravenous, terrifying beasts.

And so the day, and each successive day, continued filled with firsts of every kind. I'm glad my sons-in-law recorded the scenes. I was so engrossed in the magic of what I was seeing that I could not possibly have taken a single photo and didn't. I stared, I listened and I learned.

We sat quietly among the elegant yet mystifying giraffes. Each one on the move gave the impression of two different animals running. If you've ever seen a Chinese dragon dance ceremony, where two individuals crouch in tandem and appear to strut on four legs, while the one standing on their back or shoulders, controls the sweeping, undulating head of the dragon, you get the same image when watching live giraffes trotting on the plains.

Their heads and necks seem to float along separately from their bodies, while their cantering, horse-like torsos and legs seem to follow along trying to catch up with their heads. And yet, they are completely coordinated and graceful in the process. Even as they wrapped their long, prehensile tongues around the highest, thorny leaves of the acacia trees, from their sixteen-feet high vantage point, their big, luxuriantly lashed eyes remained fixed on us the entire time we sat beside them. They reminded us of an aristocratic court of princesses and princes aware of our presence, but not accepting us as belonging in their courtyard.

I could ramble on and on incoherently about the sights, sounds and smells of the Mara....My fishing expedition for huge catfish near a waterfall, with lion and zebra as distant companions on the far hillside... the black rhino lumbering on the plains...the Thomson gazelles leaping and frolicking in the air, with each leap setting a human world record in the Olympic track and field high-jump competition…of the vultures, each class assigned their own pecking order, in their grim but necessary role in picking each decaying carcass clean…of dung beetles, badgers and otters…of too many types of eagles and hawks to remember…of the rare sighting of a leopard with its kill wedged firmly in the fork of high branches of a tree, safe from other predators below…of screaming baboons on the hunt…of silly monkeys showing off their acrobatic skills in the trees, who John referred to as "branch managers…of the scores of "river horses," or hippos, wallowing in the Mara River, and the realization that they have been responsible for more human fatalities than any other animal in East Africa…of the hippo that charged out of the underbrush and tried to ram our Land Rover, because we were between it and the river…of the remains of a reticular python that had swallowed an antelope too large to digest.

> …of a land so full of a variety of life, that our own, civilized world back home with its cities, cars, buses, trucks, planes and trains seemed but a Hollywood set of concrete, glass, plastic and steel—a mechanized sameness—populated by wildebeest-like humanoids, who mainly migrate to and from work places in a regimented daily routine.

> But this is not meant to be a book on wildlife or animal behavior. These vignettes are just a glimpse of what we saw, yet reveal little of what we learned. What we really learned was not in what we saw, but in what it meant. It was our guide tour through the savage paradise that caused the transformation. Let me elucidate, because it is the reason I decided to write this book.

On our way back to camp, an hour later, Ladd, my other son-in-law, whispered to John that he needed John to stop the vehicle because Ladd had to make a "pit stop." Ladd disguised his urgency to respond to a call of nature by classifying the stop as a chance to "mark his territory." We all laughed as he urged John to stop the Land Rover in front of a thicket about 200 yards to the left of us, so he could do his "marking" in private.

John said that Ladd should be patient and wait a while, but Ladd protested saying that the spot he had scoped out looked good to him and that timing is everything. John smiled, encouraged Ladd to stay seated, and drove over to the "ideal spot" Ladd had selected. There in the thicket, camouflaged by the tall brown grass and brush, were seven adult lions and their cubs, who would have been noticed by Ladd just about twenty yards before reaching his so-called comfort station.

John said the lions had smelled us about twenty minutes before, and seen our approach about fifteen minutes earlier. We asked John what would have happened had we been out on one of our hikes and had come across that pride of lions in our path. After he had found a safe spot for Ladd's pit stop, he turned off the engine and gave us one of the most important lessons of our adventure.

"You need to understand animal instincts and behavior if you are to coexist with them. You need to know your environment, what you're dealing with, what to anticipate and what to do if you are surprised or challenged," John began.

"People are not normal prey for lions," he continued, "and these lions are not in the hunting mood. They are resting in the hot, afternoon sun. They wonder what we are up to but are not alarmed or upset by our presence. While it's true that there have been isolated cases of man-eating lions in the past, these incidents are exceptions to the norm."

His reassurances did little to sooth our growing apprehension about our planned hike the next morning, and we pressed him further about what we should do in a confrontation similar to that which had almost occurred for Ladd.

John said that we should stop, turn slowly and walk away at right angles to the lions. We should neither proceed toward them nor turn in retreat. When Ladd asked him why we shouldn't run away, John grinned and said: "Go ahead and run. But if you do, the rest of us will be safe, while they deal with you."

The overriding lesson of this safari was becoming clear. There is an oft-repeated cliché that I have heard ever since I was a boy. ***"It's a jungle out there."*** Every television and newspaper headline seems to shout about the perils of existence.

Bad news is always the special meal of the day. Is that because we are relieved that it happened to someone else, instead of ourselves? That we're glad we weren't the victim yesterday or today? Is it because we live lives of quiet desperation, waiting for the other shoe to drop or for the next disaster to occur? Is it that we're attracted to horrific accidents and events due to an intrinsic morbid curiosity reserved for human beings?

Every generation believes it is living at the most difficult or worst of times in history, perhaps to justify a fear of risk taking or procrastination in making tough decisions that would surely solve some of our most pressing global problems. How are we to face our deepening feelings of apprehension and fear in view of increasing global terrorism, unrest and homeland insecurity? How can we achieve survival, success and serenity in this savage paradise called life?

These are important questions and there is no single answer that fits all. The major reason we should remain informed about global, national, regional and local events is so we can respond and act effectively as individuals, families and organizations. Our need to know should lead to preparation and action, not consternation and feelings of helplessness.

The Maasai Mara is a savage paradise. Savage to the novices. A paradise to experienced travelers and residents. The same holds true with the United States, and, yes, with life itself. Life is a savage paradise. Savage to the ignorant, uneducated, unskilled, prejudiced and ill informed. A paradise to those who have learned to manage change, convert stumbling blocks into stepping stones, unhook their prejudices, remain lifelong learners and stay flexible.

John, our guide, feels comfortable and at ease in this dangerous ecosystem of East Africa. We, on the other hand, feel vulnerable, unsure and hesitant. We are naïve, in this setting, while he is wise, through knowledge and experience. We are tourists. He is the tour guide, the mentor and coach.

The analogy of the Maasai Mara being a savage paradise and likening life itself to a jungle rang a distant bell in my mind about an autobiography I had read many years before that made the same parallel. I spent the final hour on our return trip to the Cottars' camp discussing the theme with John and my family.

The book is titled *The Jungle is Neutral* and was written by Col. F. Spencer Chapman, an officer in the British army, who survived for four years in the jungle as a guerilla fighter after the fall of Malaysia to the Japanese in World War II. Cut off from all of the outside world, which heard of him only as "missing, believed killed" he lived deep in the jungle behind Japanese lines and underwent ordeals such as few men have ever lived to document.[iii] This classic non-fiction account has been compared to Lawrence of Arabia's fascinating tale, *The Seven Pillars of Wisdom*.

If Colonel Chapman were alive today, I'll wager he would respond to questions from the media on how he endured such a harrowing and impossible mission in his unflappable yet direct style. These are not his words. These are my words, interpreting my impressions of one of the most courageous individuals I have ever read about:

Media: "Sir, isn't it true that you were captured twice by the Japanese and successfully escaped from their prisons?"

Col Chapman: "That's right; they were the enemy and I needed to get out and get back to my assignment."

Media: "But sir, how did you deal with the fact that they were expert jungle fighters, and that there were scorpions, yellow fever, malaria, black mambas, incessant rain, wild tigers, leeches and undergrowth so thick it can take four hours to walk a mile?"

Col. Chapman: "I had my bouts with most of what you mentioned. Some of it I was prepared for. Some of it I learned on the job. I managed to get around by bicycle, motorcycle, dugout canoe, mostly on foot, and some of the time on my belly crawling through the jungle muck. The jungle provides drinking water, fruit and food, shelter and plenty of places to hide even if the enemy soldiers are a few yards away. I also made friends with the natives who had lived there all their lives and taught me coping skills."

Media: "Other soldiers who were in Singapore and Malaysia at the same time swear that there is nothing inviting about the jungle at all; that it is hostile, cruel and vindictive."

Col Chapman: "To me the jungle is neutral. It is your knowledge, attitude, skills and habits that see you through. The jungle is what it is. It doesn't think. It is the backdrop for your journey. Your preparation, training, resourcefulness and dedication are what count."

As we rolled into camp, I finished my story by recalling that Col. Chapman, before his exploits in Malaysia, had distinguished himself as a mountaineer in the Himalayas, as an arctic explorer in Greenland and Lapland, and had undergone extensive drilling in survival tactics in harsh environments, yet none that could compare to his four years in the jungle. The kind of grit, instincts and ingenuity displayed by Chapman, reminded me a lot of the Cottar clan. You don't come across many like them in today's western culture.

When the other guests asked us how our day went, my kids said in unison: "It's an awesome, savage paradise out there, and becoming more like a paradise every day."

Chapter Nine
Survival of the Wisest

If life is a jungle, fraught with violence, turmoil, danger lurking everywhere, insecurity and predators, how do we survive and thrive? Do we put bars on all our windows, wear body armor, hide behind double-locked doors at night? Do we carry weapons, become masters in martial arts, start pumping iron and hire security guides to shadow our every movement?

> *Or do we, ourselves, become safari guides?*

I believe we will be best prepared to face any uncertainty in the safari of life with our duffle bags filled with KASH[iv]—Knowledge, Attitudes, Skills and Habits that enable us to conquer fear of what might happen, by being equipped to anticipate, become more proactive, and to respond effectively to what happens.

While it may be true that lions are predators, and wildebeests are prey, because the lions are stronger and more fit, lions survive more by teamwork, cunning and adaptability than they do by brute force. In the human jungle of life, synergy and adaptability to change are critical to our success. Leadership used to center around power, military and economic might, and being number one. It often meant standing victoriously over a fallen adversary or competitor. As we move through the early decades of this century, where access to information is immediate and graphic, and where small bands of terrorists wreak havoc among hundreds and even thousands of innocent bystanders, it is obvious that this must change.

The leaders from now on must be champions of cooperation more often than of competition. While the power to maintain access to resources and to deter aggression will remain vital, the "survival of the fittest" mentality must give way to "survival of the wisest," a philosophy of understanding, cooperation, knowledge and reason. The real leaders will get what they want by helping others get what they want.

> Interdependence has and will continue to replace independence. The world now has too many people, too few resources, and too delicate a balance between nature and technology for leaders to operate in isolation. We will have no lasting peace until there's "a piece of pie in every mouth." The expectation of tomorrow's bigger, better pie, of which everyone will enjoy a larger piece, is what prevents people from

struggling to the end over the division of today's pie. As students of the art of self-leadership in the safari called life, we must acknowledge that we in the industrialized world are a vital but single organ of the larger body of the world's population. One segment of human beings can no longer succeed—even survive for long—without the others, including the wildlife and ecological systems that support all life upon earth. We can't continue repeating mistakes that result in extinct societies and wildlife species and expect salvation through a lottery ticket or selfish isolationism. Either we lead or we get out of the way. To wring our hands and follow is to fall hopelessly behind the emerging nations, companies and individuals—and perhaps be trampled by them.

There are two key concepts from the previous chapter that motivated me to write this book:

First, as I mentioned earlier, I didn't write it as a saga about wildlife and adventure. The discussions about the animals and interaction with them are glue hopefully to maintain the reader's interest. It was not in the "seeing" of the Maasai Mara—as in a photo album of memorable vacations—that was significant for us. It was in the "learning" from what we saw and experienced that was important. It was a kind of "Outward Bound" workshop where every event seemed to have an application to living more meaningful lives in our own world.

The second concept that inspired this work is the application of the title of Colonel Chapman's book, "The Jungle is Neutral," to the big picture in dealing with change and adversity in our own lives. It is your knowledge, attitude, skills and habits that see you through. The jungle is what it is. It doesn't think. It is the backdrop for your journey. Your preparation, training and dedication are what count.

While my daughters and their husbands went for a hike the next day, I stayed on the veranda outside my tent and began to write this book in longhand. I had written the short piece of prose as a prologue on the first evening of our safari and had brought a lined journal with me, ideal for scribbling notes and even writing a book like this one. I must admit, it was more challenging to write a non-fiction book from memory and experience, without the benefit of research material or a library.

KNOWLEDGE AS POWER

In order to move from a society of victims of change, to one of victors over change, we must change our beliefs and our behavior. The new power will be in the ability to adapt, to assume responsibility, to have a shared vision, to empower others, to negotiate successful results, and to assume control of more outcomes in our lives. The "knowledge is power" statement should be displayed in every office, factory, service center and school.

As the new tools of productivity become the combining of wireless access to the worldwide web, interactive computing and telecommunications, the people who know how to control these technologies will acquire power, while those who thought that education ends with a diploma are destined for low-paying, low-satisfaction jobs. In almost the blink of an eye, our society has passed from the industrial age to the knowledge era, in which learning and innovation—human capital skills—are keys to opportunity and advancement.

The track records of newly arrived immigrants in America seem to confirm that when you're motivated by hunger for food and knowledge, you give more in effort and service than you expect to get paid in dollars. In other words, to make it in today's global village, where the playing field is anything but level, we all need to under promise and over deliver to remain competitive and in demand.

I asked my Maasai friend and guide, John Sampeke, what the Maasai definition was for "motivation." Without hesitation, he offered the saying passed along by the elders of his clan: "When the belly is empty, you start to think." To get food you need know-how. To get knowledge you need to be motivated to learn. It's as simple as that. When you're full, you get lazy. Inner hunger gets you moving.

Many people, however, prefer to do just enough to get by. They engage in tension-relieving entertainment—game shows, reality TV, sitcoms—rather than in activities that are goal-achieving. Reading and learning seem too much like going back to school. They'd rather get home than get ahead. Actually, people would increase their learning and earning power immeasurably by spending half as much time reading as they waste staring at television.

Many of our greatest fears are based on ignorance, prejudice or lack of knowledge. My fear during the first night was a result of being in a dark tent, in a totally unfamiliar environment, complete with a cacophony of sounds that fed my imagination. Fear of the unknown becomes fear of catastrophic disaster, fear of change and fear of risk.

In my experience, there are three prevalent fears, beyond the fear regarding personal safety:

> • Fear of Rejection, which is being made a fool or failure in the sight or presence of others.
>
> • Fear of Change, which is charting unknown waters, being a pioneer, breaking tradition and sacrificing external security.
>
> • Fear of Success, which is an expression of inadequacy in feeling we perhaps don't deserve to achieve, combined with emotions of guilt when we do better than expected.

The Fear of Rejection and the Fear of Change are such dominant factors in holding people back in our society partly because of our preoccupation with "bad news" and "put downs" which discourages creative thinking and influences individuals to seek security and positions where you go with the system and don't "rock the boat;" and partly because we don't like to operate outside of our comfort zones unless forced by external circumstances.

The Fear of Success syndrome is so prevalent because we measure standards of excellence via celebrities and superstars, who appear to have talents and a charmed existence that we can never attain. We also don't like to give up the "status quo" or leave our peer group, lest they scorn us for feeling special and for wanting to move onward and upward.

In my first book, *The Psychology of Winning*, which I wrote twenty-five years ago, I told about a tribe of natives in the jungle whose family members had been dying prematurely of a strange malady for many generations. It was finally discovered that the disease was a type of encephalitis, caused by the bite of tsetse flies living in the walls of their mud homes.

The natives were offered several possible solutions. They could destroy the flies with an insecticide; they could destroy and rebuild their homes from different materials; or they could be relocated where the tsetse flies were not a problem. They chose to remain where and how they had lived for generations, and to face an early death, which was the path of least resistance and no change.

Most individuals realize that common people have become uncommonly successful by using their creative imaginations and persisting. They are familiar with biographies of those who have overcome enormous handicaps and roadblocks to become great. But they can't imagine it happening to themselves.

They resign themselves to mediocrity and even failure, wishing and envying away their lives. They develop the habit of looking back at past problems (failure-reinforcement); and imagining similar performances in the future (failure-forecasting). Because they are controlled by rejection and acceptance standards set by others, they often set their sights unrealistically high. Not really believing in the validity of their dreams, and not preparing enough for their achievement, they fall short again and again. I call this process "the curse of permanent potential."

Failure becomes set in their self-images. Just when they seem to break through, get on top, or make real progress—they blow it! In truth, the Fear of Success caused them to procrastinate the preparation and creative action necessary for success. And rationalization sets in to satisfy the subconscious feeling that "you can't expect to get ahead when you've been through what I have."

The ice cream cone was invented by a waffle vendor during the Olympic Games in St. Louis in 1904. As the crowds surged around his

The best fear busters are knowledge and action. Knowledge starts with keeping an open mind and with the hard work of self-improvement. All we learn teaches us how to think in different ways. Some of the greatest inventions and creations were born of individuals who were working on something else, when—in a flash of insight—they found the key to their masterpiece concession on that hot, summer day he ran out of cardboard plates upon which he had been serving his waffles with three different kinds of topping. With no more plates available anywhere, he thought of serving ice cream to cut his losses, but there were no cardboard bowls left in St. Louis either. At home, with the help of his wife, he made a batch of one thousand waffles, pressed them thin with a flat iron, and rolled them into a circular pattern with a point at the bottom. His waffle ice cream cones were the hit of the Olympic Games!

In the 1930s, a German immigrant in Philadelphia was trying to make a living selling knockwurst and sauerkraut in his small restaurant, having his customers hold them with inexpensive cotton gloves, since he couldn't afford plates and silverware. With most of his gloves walking out the door to be used for odd jobs at home, he had to think of something, so he split a bun and put the knockwurst and condiments inside. His clients laughed and said the knockwurst reminded them of his dachshund snoozing on the floor in the corner. In that instant, the "hot dog" was born! And for years I thought it was invented by the owner of a baseball stadium to go with the great American pastime!

In my tent, I jotted down in my journal a list of a few of the innovative ideas that I knew of wherein necessity had been the mother of invention:

• The automatic dishwasher was invented by a woman who was tired of having her china broken by the maid who washed her dishes by hand.

- Alexander Graham Bell's initial work to perfect the telephone as a listening device was motivated by his sister's hearing impairment.

- Julio Iglesias honed his guitar and singing skills while in traction during a long stay in a hospital with a badly broken leg.

- Jacques Cousteau couldn't become an astronaut because of two broken arms as a result of an auto accident, so he invented the *aqualung*—while swimming for rehabilitation—and became a legendary "aquanaut."

- Dan Gerber invented strained baby food to make his own feeding job as a young father more efficient.

- Ole Evinrude invented the outboard motor, because he couldn't row his boat fast enough to keep the ice cream from melting that he purchased for his girlfriend on the other side of the lake.

- Tom Monaghan, founder of Domino's Pizza, developed a box to keep his delivered pizza hot so he could service college students in Ypsilanti, Michigan who got hungry as they did their all-night, last-minute term papers and crammed for final exams.

- When my friend and neighbor, Ray Kroc, franchised the McDonald's hamburger chain, his major goal was to sell his line of multi-mixer malt machines.

- Fred Smith's idea for a Memphis-hub air package delivery service, that became the Federal Express success story, emanated from a term paper project for a college class. It didn't even earn Fred a high grade!

I've often wondered why so many of these incredible breakthrough products and services come from outside the industry involved. It's got to have something to do with "group think" and the notion that experts within the industry or company would have invented it already, if it was a good idea. When you fail to challenge your own assumptions with new knowledge and a positive, receptive attitude, you're bound to lose out to the competition. I've had personal experience with entrepreneurs like Michael Dell and I marvel at the youthful brilliance and risk-oriented enthusiasm and passion that he, and others like the founders of Microsoft, Yahoo and Google, exude on a daily basis. They definitely see opportunities disguised as problems.

Just as I was about to add another 30 or 40 inventions that had been inspired either as solutions to problems, or as side issues to the main event, John Sampeke strode up the path to greet me outside my tent. I shared with him some of the innovations I knew of that had been stumbling blocks turned into stepping stones. He suggested that since it was a cool day, I should join himself and my family for a hike on the Mara to see what we could see and we could brainstorm as we strolled.

I told him I was having concerns as to how to bridge my writings on knowledge, attitudes, skills and habits into our environment here at the Cottars 1920s safari camp. He smiled and said, "Put your boots on and I'll show you." And off we went for a walk on the wild side. I'm still a little nervous on these hikes out in the bush in Africa. Even though John Sampeke or Calvin Cottar are leading the way, armed with their rifles and there is a Maasai warrior with a spear following behind, what if we were to meet a pride of fifteen lions or two buffalos with a bad hair day, or a rhino with an attitude? I didn't voice my concerns since I wanted John, Calvin and my kids to think I was like Mel Gibson in *Braveheart*.

When you come to Kenya, you must go on a walking safari with Calvin Cottar or John Sampeke. There is no question that each is the best in his particular specialty. The day we went with Calvin, we were amazed with his sensory awareness at every level and total understanding of his environment and virtually every aspect of animal behavior.

He knew when the cheetah was ready to hunt. He could tell by the depths of the paw and hoof prints in the mud, who had been drinking at or crossing the river, and how long ago. He could easily differentiate the calling cards and territorial markings of eland, zebra, wildebeest, lion, leopard, hyena, buffalo, rhino, warthog, Thomson's gazelle, giraffe, elephant and baboon. He could see with the naked eye what we could barely distinguish through binoculars. Calvin knew where you could walk and where you shouldn't; what plants were edible or productive and which were not. His knowledge of the Maasai Mara, where several generations of his family had lived and worked for over eighty years, was so extensive that you felt completely at ease and confident with him by your side. To him the Mara is much more a paradise than the savage frontier it first appears to the novice tourist. With Calvin along, you felt comfortable, excited and safe. Isn't that what the safari of life is supposed to feel like?

With John Sampeke at our side that afternoon, we felt the same, with the exception that John enjoys quizzing his clients like a *Jeopardy* or *Family Feud* game show host. When my grandchildren, Alex and Alissa, came the following year, he turned every walk and drive into a summer camp field trip. He would tell them that they needed a perfect score on the wildlife test for the day, or no dessert after dinner.

Then he would quiz them: "O.K., so we saw the big five today, which are?" And the kids would reply in unison, "Lion, elephant, rhino, leopard and buffalo!" "Great job," he would exclaim. "Now, what are the *little five* we saw today?" These didn't come as easily to Alex and Alissa, who hesitated a little, "Uh, there is the Lion ant, the Elephant shrew, the Rhino beetle, the Leopard tortoise, and the Buffalo .....Uh, some kind of little bird." "That's pretty good, kids" John remarked. "Four out of five is fair enough for today, but look at that wildlife book we went over with all the birds, insects and animals and see if you can see the name of the Buffalo bird."

The knowledge we gained on our hike with our guide, John, was like survival training for life itself. He showed us a special kind of bush that had green pods for blossoms. When John opened some of the pods, he introduced us to an entire ant colony where each pod of the bush had a different function. There was a nursery for the babies, tended by nurses; there was a dining area, a sleeping area, a work area and even an ant cemetery. John remarked that we often pass miracles of life, unnoticed, when we hurry rather than observe.

I had a little trouble with my contact lenses from the blowing dust while we were walking. John found another bush with soft orange berries. He plucked two and told me to squeeze the contents in each eye, since I had forgotten to bring my re-wetting drops with me. The liquid from the berries soothed my eyes, and relieved the dryness from my lenses. He smiled and said: "Very much like what you call, Visine, isn't it?

John picked leaves that made your skin tingle when you rubbed them lightly on your face. They were used for exfoliating the dead skin and cleaning the pores. He picked some fragrant *leleshwa* leaves from another bush-like tree and suggested that we put some under each arm as a natural deodorant, if we felt the need.

One of the most amazing lessons we learned occurred when my daughter, Debi, suffered a deep scratch on her arm from the thorn of an acacia tree in a dense thicket we were passing through. Since we didn't have a first aid kit with us, John applied some antiseptic sap from a tree to her wound and then demonstrated what he would have done had the scratch required suturing. Nearby there was a battalion of army ants on the march, and John reached down and grabbed a few of the larger "sentry" ants that were guarding the flanks of the moving ant army. They had big pincers and John applied the pincers to Debi's arm with the deftness of a surgeon sewing up an incision. He said that by placing the pincers of the sentry ants all along the scratch, the wound would be closed sufficiently until we got back to camp to take other action if it had been more serious.

The entire walk was a continuing education experience in awareness of our environment, in using the resources available at the time, in innovating and coping to meet unforeseen challenges and surprises, and the ability to solve problems, while at the same time converting them into opportunities to grow on and learn from.

I could write another book about John Sampeke's first visit to America. After my first safari in Kenya, I had invited him to enjoy an "urban safari" in the United States as my guest. If I expected a movie sequel to *Crocodile Dundee Comes to New York*, I was in for another lesson. His knowledge, attitude, skills and habits served him well. His observation, spotting and tracking skills were evident from the moment I picked him up at the San Diego airport.

As I marveled at the wealth of knowledge possessed by our guide, John, which enabled him to view the Maasai Mara as welcoming, rather than foreboding, I wondered how he would fare in my environment in Southern California or in other industrialized cities and countries. I soon found that he was better prepared to survive and thrive in his world and our world, than I would ever be to survive and thrive in his. When he came to America to visit me the following summer, he was never a "tourist" and ever a "guide."

John noticed that the left rear wheel on a truck was shimmying and suggested that we hail the driver and tell him to fix it. I commented that we don't do that on Southern California freeways. He shrugged and wondered why not. He noticed all the different license plates, with their slogans, vanity names, colors for different states, and saw that each had a separate expiration date. He tracked the pigeons on the freeway overhangs, the black birds on the phone wires, the seagulls by the ocean, the hawks soaring over the canyons, and the sparrows in the trees. He observed the speeders, the slow pokes, the "road ragers" and the road hogs. He was a combination of a radar and a sponge. He didn't miss a thing and displayed the curiosity of a child in a toy store.

At Sea World he devoted more than half-an-hour studying the manatees, observing that some had scars from being run over by outboard motors in the Florida everglades. He spent an hour comparing the thrust power of the killer whales with the leaping ability of lions, and was awed that these beautiful ocean mammals could propel themselves over twelve feet into the air from a short run underwater.

We didn't visit the world famous San Diego Zoo for obvious reasons. As wonderful a facility as it is to give people the opportunity to visit wildlife, it would have been a sad experience for a man of the Maasai to see perhaps a preview of coming attractions of what could happen to the people and animals of East Africa as their territories are invaded, parceled, bulldozed and fenced. Instead, we went to Disneyland, on a Saturday that broke all previous attendance records. Even with our computerized reservations on our tickets designating the times we should plan to be at each attraction or ride, the waiting times were nearly an hour at each location.

The standing in long lines in the hot sun didn't faze John. We didn't bother trying to get something to eat, because the waits at the restaurants were almost an hour as well. In the middle of the day, surrounded by over one hundred fifty thousand individuals, thirty thousand strollers, and at least ten thousand fussy infants and toddlers, John smiled at me and commented prophetically: "Just like the great wildebeest migration in Kenya!"

Naturally, John enjoyed the *It's A Small World* ride best of all, because it featured harmony among all the different cultures around the globe. When I asked him how he enjoyed the overall Disneyland experience, he said that it was very nice, but didn't seem to give the families much time to explore or spend quality time with each other. He wondered why we Americans always seem to congregate in masses in close quarters in parks, in arenas and even on beaches. He thought that getting away from crowds would be more pleasant than seeking more crowds in one's free time. And he noticed that even at Disneyland, everyone was in a rush to see how many rides they could manage in one visit, so typical of tourists who come to Kenya to scurry around taking as many photos as possible, before moving on to the next watering hole on their jam-packed agenda.

John and I went to the Museums of Man and Natural History in San Diego's Balboa Park, and both noticed the similarities of tools, weapons, and abodes of ancient societies throughout the world. At Pepperdine University in Malibu, we had lunch with the Chancellor in his private dining room and I couldn't believe that John was as relaxed and comfortable in that setting as he was on our hikes on the Mara plains.

Nothing seemed to faze John, but he later told me that perhaps the most exciting event of his trip came when he had left me in San Diego to join another friend in Michigan. In addition to the experience of being in

114

a Midwestern environment, very much different from Southern California, he said he really enjoyed all the boating activities on some of Michigan's wonderful lakes. He said, "I found water skiing to be a lot of fun, but a little challenging until you get good at it." He said that first he watched others doing it, and then tried to imitate their techniques. I said, "So were you nervous when you first tried to stand up on the skis?" "Not really, at that time," he replied. "Only after I fell and let go of the rope." "Why was that?" I queried. "Because I don't know how to swim!" he laughed.

Here was a Maasai who had not learned how to swim before, because there was no cause to living out on the Mara of East Africa. Yet, he took up water skiing because the risk didn't seem that great, reasoning that the life jacket everyone wore would keep him afloat. So he didn't see any need to advise his friends that he couldn't swim.

We all yearn to shape our own lives, fashion our own destinies. But most of us find ourselves in the same dilemma from our teens onward. How do we really want to spend our days? What choices should we make? What can we do that will fill our lives with meaning and bring us the adventure and rewards we seek? How do we know we've chosen the right career and the proper goals? Who should be our role models now?

These heavy questions can't be taken lightly nor formularized. We mustn't let our first jobs after high school or college determine our lives from there ever after. Nor should we let our parents, professors, or friends

> There is no question that knowledge, attitude, skills and habits conquer fear. In the next chapter, we'll discuss why knowledge must be internalized through skills and habits to make surviving and thriving a reflex actions that enable us to remain calm and in control when we are under pressure. Perhaps the greatest reason for becoming lifelong learners is to understand our own talents, core passions and limitations. To know ourselves and to grow in that knowledge is the path to self-fulfillment.

choose our careers—or let money alone make our long-range decisions. Most people allow their jobs or geography—external factors—to set their courses. This is like the chicken in the chicken-and-egg conundrum. Starting with the egg—the internal factor is much more likely to assure success. We must take the first step toward meaningful goals and a life strategy by being true to ourselves.

The meaning of this inquiry can be understood by stepping back to look at the whole person. This self-assessment spawns another big question. Why are most people better equipped for and more motivated by their hobbies than for their life's work?

If it weren't for time, money or circumstances how would you choose to spend your life? What do you enjoy doing most that you're not doing now? What special talents, skills and knowledge do you have that you're not fully employing. What is your core passion, that has little to do with your financial pension?

By retaining your inner hunger for knowledge, and by dedicating yourself to becoming a lifelong learner, you will find the answers to those questions and more. The more you learn, the less you will fear. You will welcome risk and create your own inner security.

The acquisition of knowledge is a lifelong experience, not a collection of facts. Not long ago, what you learned in school was largely all you needed to learn to guarantee employment; you could rely on that knowledge for the rest of your life. With access to information expanding exponentially, this is no longer true. Hundreds of scientific papers are published daily. Every thirty seconds, some new technology company produces yet another innovation. Your formal education has a very short shelf life, perhaps only about eighteen months.

In this modern-day jungle, with ever more to know, leaders need—and many are demonstrating—a new attitude toward learning. Although most are too busy managing to spend much time in classrooms, they continue learning by teaching themselves, absorbing new ideas and knowledge largely on the run.

> Their love of learning springs from a natural curiosity and their risk-taking nature affects the way they learn. It inspires them to dig deeper, to want to know not just how but also "why." Interestingly enough, the people who do know "why" often have many people with "know-how" working for them

Thus lifelong learning means far more than formal classroom knowledge. In a world in which working with people is essential, it also means deepening your understanding of yourself and others. In today's fast-forward world, it is difficult to distinguish personal development skills from business skills. Executives who believe they have sufficient educations are on a fast track to personal obsolescence.

> Lifelong learning, once a luxury for the few, has become absolutely vital to continued success.

But while there are dangers in trying to become a leader without thoroughly knowing your field, there are also dangers in thinking of yourself as an expert—especially the danger of losing your sense of wonder. Instead of being driven by curiosity, you become driven to defend what you've previously researched, invented, created, marketed or published. Reciting safe answers now, you stop saying the liberating words, "I don't know."

Leaders who are constantly learning throughout their lives never forget they always have more to learn. Although their knowledge and experience may have made them teachers, they continue to think of themselves as students. The most compelling reason to avoid thinking like an expert even while continuing to acquire expertise is that your assumptions may prejudice and hinder your ability to generate and work with new ideas. In the next chapter we'll also mention some specific strategies and guideposts which will enable us to better manage change in a world in which the only rule is change.

ATTITUDE IS YOUR LOCK OR KEY

I've spent the past forty years of my career searching for answers to help other human beings enjoy happy, meaningful and productive lives. I have broken bread with some of the most famous sports, media, business, political, entertainment, scientific and religious icons of our times, and interviewed and studied many lesser known, but perhaps even more successful men and women, who were so busy setting an example as positive role models worth emulating, they rarely sought fame or notoriety.

> The one outstanding character trait—among many others such as integrity, determination, focus, persistence and graciousness—that seems to be a common denominator in every winning person I have encountered is an attitude of positive belief or optimism.

Some time ago, Billy Graham invited me to speak at a rally of about thirty thousand people. Before the event, Dr. Graham relaxed, as he often did, in a small trailer behind the arena. We shook hands. "So, Denis," he said, his penetrating eyes boring into mine. "How many lives have you changed in your career?" I blinked but smiled back. "I believe I've changed one that I know of, Billy. My own."

"Me too," he replied, eyes now twinkling. "I believe the only life I've changed is mine. But I keep on trying to become a positive influence for others because I believe in what I say and I believe in what I'm doing—don't you?"

I nodded. My work, I said, is based on a deep core-belief system; my very soul is in it. He reminded me that when we talk about faith and attitude, we must refer to what he calls the greatest book ever written and the greatest teacher of the ages on the subject. He summed it up by saying, "Go your way—and as you have believed, so it will be done unto you."

That simple statement cuts both ways, like a two-edged sword or a lock and key. Belief is the key that can unlock the right door for everyone, the means for getting rid of the lock that imprisons people, keeping them from ever knowing success. It is a power everyone has but few consciously use. No individual possesses more of it than any other. Therefore, the question isn't whether we have faith, it's whether we use it correctly.

> Belief as a positive force is the promise of realizing things hoped for and unseen. As a negative force, it is the premonition of our deepest fears and unseen darkness. (Many people lead lives of quiet desperation, having most of their 365 nights each year spent in anxiety as I had on my first safari night in my tent.) There's no such thing as an absence of faith; it's always one kind or another— optimism, or cynicism and despair.

Just as our Maasai friend John, as an elder in his village, has been granted the powers to engage in healing ceremonies and engage in casting spells, so do each of us have ingrained beliefs that greatly influence our outcomes and those of others who look to us for guidance. Much has been written for centuries about the self-fulfilling prophecy. A self-fulfilling prophecy is a statement that is neither true nor false but that may become true if believed. I have lectured and written much about the fact that the mind can't distinguish between things real and things vividly imagined—which is why faith and belief are so important.

For example, when our fears and worries turn into anxiety, we suffer distress. Distress activates our endocrine system, changing the production of hormones and antibodies. Our immune system becomes less active; our resistance levels are lowered; we become more vulnerable to bacteria, viruses and other ever-present hazards. I've long said that ulcers aren't what you eat, they're what's eating you. There is evidence that some forms of asthma are psychosomatic—more related to a smothering relationship with a doting parent ("smother love") than to outside allergens. In some cases, pictures of goldenrod we're enough to bring on attacks of hay fever. In many cases, what we expect to happen, what we believe will happen, *makes* it happen.

The powerful loneliness and hurt associated with what we call a broken heart can indeed lead to heart problems. There is also an apparent link between bottled-up emotions and the growth of some cancerous tumors. Some splitting headaches might be precipitated by being pulled in opposite directions. A rigid personality and suppressed rage have been identified as factors in some cases of arthritis.

> *Faith is a house of many beliefs and it's time we put the house in order. How does your lifestyle—your expectations and your forecasting—affect your own health and well-being?*

I share with many audiences a true story about a man named Nick. (A reenactment of this story on video is available through American Media in Des Moines, Iowa.) Nick, a strong, healthy railroad yardman, goes along reasonably well with his fellow workers and was consistently reliable on the job. However, he was a deep pessimist who invariably feared the worst. One spring day, the train crews were told they could quit an hour early in honor of the foreman's birthday. When the other workmen left the site, Nick, the notorious worrier, was accidentally locked in an isolated refrigerator boxcar that was in the yard for repairs.

He panicked. He shouted and banged until his voice went hoarse and his fists were bloody. The noises, if anyone heard them, were assumed to be coming from a nearby playground or from other trains backing in and out of the yard.

Nick reckoned the temperature in the car was zero degrees. "If I can't get out," he thought, "I'll freeze to death." He found a cardboard box. Shivering uncontrollably, he scrawled a message to his wife and family. "So cold, body's getting numb. If I could just go to sleep. These may be my last words."

The next morning, the crew slid open the boxcar's heavy doors and found Nick's body. An autopsy revealed that every physical sign indicated he had frozen to death. But the car's refrigeration unit was inoperative. The temperature inside was about 61 degrees and there was plenty of fresh air. Nick's fear had become a self-fulfilling prophecy.

Scientists have known for many decades that hormones play an important role in regulating some of our biological processes. Adrenaline enables us to "fight or flee" in the face of danger, and to get "up" for physical performances. Insulin regulates blood sugar levels. We have learned that our bodies manufacture morphine-like hormones to block pain and give us a natural high. These natural endorphins can be fifty to ninety times more powerful than morphine.

No doubt you're familiar with the placebo effect. (Placebo literally means "I shall please.") Placebos are inert substances given to some volunteers in a given study while other volunteers are treated with experimental drugs—whose effect is tested by measuring the difference in response to the powerless placebo and to the drug. Some of a group of volunteers who had just had their wisdom teeth extracted were given morphine to alleviate their pain; the others swallowed a placebo they believed to be a powerful pain killer. Many of the placebo recipients said they experienced dramatic relief from their pain, believing they had been given morphine too. However, when a drug that blocks the effects of the natural endorphin was given to them, the pain returned almost immediately. This test, and many others, have confirmed something very important: When a patient believes he or she has been given a pain reliever, the brain releases chemicals to substantiate that belief. In short, the placebo effect is an act of faith.

> *Optimism is an incurable condition in the person with faith. Optimists believe that most disease, distress, dysfunction, and disturbance can be remedied. Optimists also are prevention and wellness oriented. Their thoughts and actions are focused on solutions, health and success. They concentrate on positive outcomes and rewards, rather than the penalties of failure.*

Many books have been written about the mind as healer. One of my favorites is *The Anatomy of an Illness: As Perceived by the Patient*, a national bestseller about twenty-five years ago, but as relevant today as it was then. It was written by former *Saturday Review* editor, Norman Cousins, who was hospitalized with an extremely rare, crippling disease. When conventional medicine failed to improve his condition and he was diagnosed as incurable, Cousins checked out of the hospital. Being aware of the harmful effects that negative emotions can have on the human body, Cousins reasoned that the reverse also might be true. He decided to dwell on becoming well again.

He borrowed a movie projector and prescribed his own treatment plan, consisting of Marx Brothers motion pictures and old "Candid Camera" reruns on film. He studied all aspects of his disease and with the help of his physician, learned what would have to take place in his body to make it "right" again. In his book he recounts that he "made the joyous discovery that ten minutes of genuine belly laughter would give me at least two hours of pain-free sleep." What had seemed to be a progressively debilitating, fatal cellular disease was reversed and, in time, Cousins almost completely recovered.

His experiences have appeared in the *New England Journal of Medicine* and, in addition to UCLA where he became a faculty member for many years, thirty-four medical schools have included his work in their instructional materials.

Thoughts and images do have an unmistakable, measurable physical reaction. What the mind harbors the body manifests in some way. Very recent studies have determined that the placebo effect is much more powerful than previously imagined. So be careful what you believe and pretend—it may come to pass.

I slept soundly on that August night in the Kenya highlands, hoping I could interpret the handwritten scrawls in my journal when I returned home to my word processor. Had I adequately described my own beliefs about *The Survival of the Wisest* versus *The Survival of the Fittest* approaches to life? Would they resonate and make sense to the reader, when this work was published, and not just seem like a pouring forth of random thoughts from a man, sans research material, in a kerosene-lighted tent? I didn't know.

> What I felt strongly about was that wisdom is the time-grown ability to convert a negative event into a learning experience that can create a positive future outcome. Wisdom is learning from your own mistakes, so you don't repeat them. Wisdom is learning from your own successes, so you can continue and compound them. Wisdom is learning from others mistakes, so you don't have to personally experience them. And, wisdom is learning from others' successes, so you can minimize "trial and error" time and exposure, which can save years of frustration and add years of productive living.

It took a walk on the wild side to crystallize my own application of these principles and to realize I still had a lot of "wising up" to do on my own life safari.

127

Chapter Ten
Guideposts in the
Savage Paradise

With only two days remaining on my first safari, I made myself a check-off list of skills I needed to develop around a knowledge-base to graduate from being a cautious "tourist" in life to becoming a courageous "guide" for myself and family. The next-to-last morning I wrote:

- ☐ *Know your environment*
- ☐ *Know the participants*
- ☐ *Know your own strengths and limitations*
- ☐ *Know your purpose and inner motives*
- ☐ *Know that others have a different agenda, often hidden*
- ☐ *Know that there are givers and takers, prey and predators*
- ☐ *Know how to be a giver, but not a prey for predators*
- ☐ *Know enough to say "I don't know."*
- ☐ *Know that change is the rule, but not the ruler*

To complete the KASH formula we discussed in the previous chapter, we need to add Skills and Habits to Knowledge and Attitude. The reason skills and habits are critical to surviving and thriving in the savage paradise of life is that we live in a fast-forward world with more changes in one day than in a decade of our grandparents' lives.

> *Our society's current condition reminds me of the opening line in Charles Dicken's "A Tale of Two Cities", "It was the best of times, it was the worst of times."*

It is the worst of times as measured by some aspects of our national life, especially our growing insecurities regarding terrorism at home; our obsession with skin-deep pleasures, our eroding moral standards and violent entertainment; our born-in-America mentality that suggests entitlement to prosperity and being blind to the reality that the rising expectations of developing nations and the fact that newly arrived immigrants in our country are willing to give more in service than they expect in payment; our dependence on fossil fuel energy, combined with our polluting of our own habitat; and the growing global unrest between "haves" and "have nots" and between religious and ethnic sects. It is the best of times because we have instant access to knowledge that can free us all from the slavery of ignorance and its twin brother, prejudice.

These *are* troubled times. That's why many people bide their time and hope that the future will favor them with a brighter outlook, including a whopping check from the Powerball lottery. Others would gladly turn back the hands of time to "the good old days" when you could leave your doors unlocked, when gasoline was a dollar a gallon, and you didn't have to remove half your clothing on your way to the boarding area to catch a plane for business or a fun vacation.

Today if you pick up the newspaper and turn to the editorial page, you might read something like this:

> The world is too big for us. Too much going on, too many crimes, too much violence and excitement. Try as you will you get behind in the race, in spite of yourself. It's an incessant strain, to keep pace...and still, you lose ground. Science empties its discoveries on you so fast that you stagger beneath them in hopeless bewilderment. The political world is news seen so rapidly you're out of breath trying to keep up with who's in and who's out. Everything is high pressure. Human nature can't endure much more!

This editorial reads like it could have appeared last week in *The Washington Post* or *Los Angeles Times*. But it actually was published nearly one hundred seventy-five years ago, on June 16, 1833 in *The Atlantic Journal*. That was back in "the good old days." What does it mean to you and me? What can we learn from this? I believe this simple, tattered editorial, nearly two centuries old, teaches us one of the secrets in how to survive and thrive in the savage paradise called life.

Looking back in history, we need to remind ourselves that the "good old days" had some very bad conditions. World wars, global plagues, and mostly tyrants ruling condescending servants, killing or imprisoning any and all who spoke of differing beliefs. There is so much emphasis today, however, on what's going wrong in the world at present, because television is our window to experience tragedy up front, close and personal, that had the first product of electricity been the electric chair instead of the light bulb, we'd all be warned by the tabloid media not to plug in our toasters and cell phones!

As we look back into history, we can always find the worst of times and best of times. I'm grateful I didn't have to take a bath in a huge pan, using water that was heated over a wood- or coal-burning stove. In that era we bathed in the same water as those in the family who went before us. If you followed your uncle and, as fate would have it, he was a pig farmer, instead of getting ring around the collar, you got ring around the person! I smiled to myself about that image as I took my solar-powered hot shower in my tent on the Maasai Mara.

Being a confirmed optimist, I told John on our game drive that morning that I looked forward to living long enough to see motor vehicles powered by advanced battery packs for the short runs to and from offices and shopping. And for the longer runs, using a car, bus or truck powered by safe hydrogen engines. The exhaust from our future highway vehicles will most likely be pure oxygen and steam, which are the by-products from burning liquid hydrogen. In effect, there will be tens of millions of rolling vacuum cleaners sucking the smog out of Los Angeles, Mexico City, and Bangkok, and replacing it with air cleaner than the air above Mount Kenya. A big semitrailer will roar down the freeway belching clouds of pure oxygen out of its stacks. There will be a sticker on the back of the truck with a new slogan: "Teamsters for Clean Air!"

John said he believed it had to happen if we are to survive on this planet. And we both agreed that "the good old days are here and now." Otherwise we would go through life looking through the rear view mirror at the good times we had in the past, playing up how awful conditions are today in order to justify own lack of innovation and achievement. Because our current generation does not study history, in order not to repeat the mistakes that were made there, most people don't learn from history that problems are normal and most prevalent during changing times. By complaining about the cruel world and sticking their heads into the sands of a host of inane reality TV shows, they never really have to roll up their sleeves and solve their problems. They can blame their problems on the current administration in Washington or in their state capitol and pursue the new society's diversion—Escape Goat. Escape Goat is a game in which everyone runs and hides and tries to find someone else willing to be "It."

In my lectures and seminars, I recite a little original rhyme that sums up my own rhetoric on the subject:

"If you're feeling blue, there's nothing wrong with you. The prudent thing to do, is find someone to sue!"

So what are you and I supposed to do in this "best of times, worst of times" scenario?   I believe we need to develop some coping skills and some new healthy habits layered over the old unhealthy habits we have learned by observation, imitation and repetition.

TURNING STRESS INTO SUCCESS

I've had many meaningful relationships in my life, but my most significant role models have been my grandmother, Mabel Ostrander; Dr. Jonas Salk—developer of the first effective polio vaccine; Billy Graham, who I mentioned previously; Anne Morrow Lindbergh, humanitarian author and wife of Charles Lindbergh, who made the first trans-Atlantic flight; Dr. Myron Wentz, the leading microbiologist in human cellular nutrition; Wilma Rudolph, former Olympic multi-gold-medalist; Viktor Frankel, the Holocaust survivor and psychiatrist who wrote the classic *Man's Search for Meaning*; and Dr. Hans Selye, the acknowledged "father of stress research."   At this writing, all but Billy Graham and

Myron Wentz are gone, but all continue to influence my life significantly.

I benefited greatly from my intense friendship with Dr. Hans Selye who died in 1982. As a young doctor who emigrated from Central Europe to Canada in the 1930s, he first borrowed the English word *stress* from physics to describe the body's responses to everything from viruses and cold temperature, to emotions such as fear and anger. Dr. Selye's definition of stress, three quarters of a century old, is still the best explanation of what it really is.

> *"Stress is the body's nonspecific response to any demand placed on it, whether that demand is pleasant or not."*

I always considered Hans Selye to be a little boy, with bright, curious eyes, inside the frail body of an older man. We served on the board and faculty of the International Society for Advanced Education together, along with Jonas Salk, and I was so fascinated with his pioneering stress research that I made many trips to visit Dr. Selye at the Institute of Experimental Medicine and Surgery in Montreal. Over a period of five years, I audiotaped our interviews, which I consider to be among my most priceless personal possessions. I have always been one to collect and share treasured moments, rather than material objects or things. My ideal living quarters would be a library, with floor to ceiling bookshelves and a ladder on wheels I could navigate throughout the great room in search of gems of wisdom on printed pages, day or night.

In my conversations with Hans Selye, we often discussed the two faces of stress. He observed that sitting in a dentist's chair or passionate kissing can be equally stressful—however, not equally agreeable. He said that when a mother suddenly hears that her son has died in battle, she will show all the biochemical changes characteristic of stress. Under stress, there is a need for bodily movement. In addition, the mucous lining of the stomach starts to dissolve, the body loses weight, the adrendal glands lose their store of hormones, and the individual suffers from insomnia. These are the non-specific responses. However, the specific effect of that news is great pain and suffering.

Hypothetically, what would happen if this same son walked into her living room a few years later, perfectly healthy. The news had been false; he had been missing in action, as a POW instead of a fatality. The specific effects of this experience are very pleasant. However, the nonspecific stress is just about the same as in the case of the bad news. It is not the physical stimulus that makes the difference; it is the attitude with which we take it!

One evening when we were sitting in Dr. Selye's study, I told him my father had given me my first skills lesson in how to cope with stress, at my age of nine. My dad and mom separated shortly thereafter, and my brother, sister and I didn't have much contact with him throughout the remainder of our lives. I still never forgot what he told me on that one particular night.

When I went to bed, he came in and sat with me for a while for a chat. I don't know whether it was because he went away when we were young, but those were very special moments when a parent and child can bond quietly at bedtime and share some precious inspiration to sleep on. When he left my room, after tucking me in, he would "blow" out my light, as if by magic. I didn't see his hand flick off the switch from behind his back. All I remember is that it seemed like he had some secret power to blow it out like a candle on a cake.

After my room became dark he would say softly, "Goodnight, my son. Always remember that when your light goes out, it goes out all over the world. Light and life are in the eyes of the beholder. How you see it is how it will be, no matter what others say. When you are happy, the world is a great place. When you are sad, it is a lonely place. Keep your eyes open and bright to the light in the darkness. Life is what *you* make it…it makes little difference what is happening…it is how *you* take it that counts!"

I told Hans Selye that those words my father had given me as a boy had stayed with me all of my adult life, like a beacon in the fog. Dr. Selye told me that my father's philosophy matched his own. He said that he had condensed twenty years of research into a 300-page book called *The Stress of Life.* When McGraw-Hill told him his explanations were still too long and complicated, he boiled his research into a ten-page summary. When the editor told him it was still too complex, he decided to make it short and simple enough for everyone to understand:

> *"Fight for your highest attainable aim, but never put up resistance in vain."*

What that little slogan meant to me is easily illustrated by my reaction to aircraft or flight scheduling problems when I am traveling. I am one of American and Delta Airlines most frequent fliers, having logged millions of miles of airtime on my global lecture tours. When a flight is delayed or canceled for one reason or another, I am the first off the plane or on my phone to make alternate arrangements. I go to great effort to get where I'm going, by every means possible. If it turns out that I have exhausted all options in getting to my destination—such as flying back toward my original city, by flying well out of the way, by renting a car or taking a limo to a city where I can make a connection, by chartering a private plane to get me there, or a bus or a train—I find a hotel room to relax or work, eat a slow meal, and call ahead saying I'll be late. I never get upset by circumstances I cannot control and therefore never put up resistance in vain.

Here are some rules and skills courtesy of Dr. Selye and myself to convert the stresses in your life to success and serenity:

1. Find a lifestyle that fits your personality and personal stress tolerance level. Most of us fit into two main categories. I thought about these categories while on a game drive during our safari to the Maasai Mara in Kenya. There are the human "cheetahs" who are happiest with life in the fast lane. Then, there are the human "tortoises" who definitely are more attuned to a more paced, tranquil environment. (It was humorous to watch lion cubs trying to figure out how to get inside of that hard shell to its occupant, who knew when to move and when to rest.) If you feed a cheetah so he doesn't need to run, he will atrophy and after a while he won't be able to run. But if you try to teach a turtle to run as fast as a cheetah, you would kill it.

Most of us are trying to be cheetahs. We charge through our lives as if life were a race to finish first. The real mission is to find a purpose that we can respect. It needs to be *our* goal—not the goal of our parents, or our friends, but our own personal, individual goal. One way to determine whether you are on the right track is to define your own meaning of "work." We all seem to clamor for shorter working hours and larger incomes. What is work and what is enjoyment?

If work is what you have to do, then enjoyment is what you want to do. A professional fisherman who has been out to sea and is exhausted coming home will do some gardening and relax in the evening. The professional gardener, conversely, probably will go out fishing to get away from his work. Although we all need diversion, you must be certain that you enjoy your profession sufficiently to call it a "play" profession. I know many scientists, artists, health professionals, athletes, teachers, humanitarians and coaches who have said they don't classify what they do as work, although they are up at five each morning and are involved in their professions up to twelve hours every day. This kind of attitude is possible for all of us to develop more, by bringing more of our natural talents and core passions into our daily routines. We also need to understand that intrinsic motivation, the inner fire, is more enjoyable and lasting than extrinsic motivation, or that motivated by externals such as money and position.

2. Control your emotional demonstrations by recognizing situations as being either life-threatening or non-life-threatening. Respond, rather than react. There is a psychological myth that venting your anger is the healthy thing to do. We see negative role models do this every night on television and our younger generation, particularly, is getting the wrong message. The problem with venting anger is that you can't take back what you said or did to the person receiving it. And it becomes habit forming. Ask any wife or mother who have been a victim or a husband's or a child's tantrums. Ask any child who has been abused by habitually irate parents. *Anger can result from threatened values.* Most people who display a lot of anger have low self-esteem and view every divergent opinion as a personal threat. Terrorists certainly are full of self-loathing and have bought into the myth that they will be worthy martyrs only when they have sacrificed their own lives in the act of destroying innocent victims.

Within our body there are two types of chemical messengers: the so-called messengers of peace (the doves), which tell the tissues not to fight because it's not worth it; and the messengers of war (the hawks) which tell the body to destroy invading foreign substances and fight.

The messengers of peace are called "syntoxic" hormones—from the Greek "syn" meaning together—that tell the tissues to take it easy and you won't get sick. The messengers of war are called "catatoxic" hormones. Their mission is to search for and destroy dangerous invaders that are life-threatening. They stimulate the production of various enzymes which destroy substances in the body. The problem with people who react to everyday life confrontations with this "fight or flight" catatoxic reaction is that they are spending their energies on the wrong causes.

All of us have a "stress" savings account deposited in our bodies as our life force. The object is to spend it wisely over the longest time span possible. The difference between our "stress" savings account and a normal bank account is that we won't make many deposits into the "stress" account as we get older. We basically make withdrawals. The reason most people age at such different rates is that our society is full of "big spenders" who overreact to harmless, petty or easy to deal with circumstances as if they were life-or-death matters. We see it every day on our highways, in our airports, at sporting events, on our school playgrounds, in our offices and in our homes.

True maturity is in knowing when to behave syntoxically and when to react catatoxically. If you go out in the evening and meet a drunk, he may shower you with insults. Recognizing that he is a harmless, obnoxious drunk, you take a syntoxic attitude and pass him by, saying nothing. He's so out of it, he can't attack his own bar stool. You adapt to the annoyance and no trouble results.

What if, instead, you react with a surge of adrenalin that stimulates pulse, respiration and blood pressure. Your digestive processes turn off at once and the protective lining of the stomach starts to dissolve, as all of the blood rushes to your battle zones. Your coagulation chemistry prepares to resist wounds with quick clotting. The alarm system is in red alert.

Even if you don't actually fight, you can have a serious or fatal heart attack. In this case, the stress of preparing for battle is what killed you. Consider that carefully. Who was the murderer? The drunk didn't touch you. How many people are killing themselves or aging prematurely because they are not aware of the consequences of their behavior?

By not being aware, you also could have misunderstood the situation in an opposite sense. You observe an individual displaying suspicious or irrational behavior and you mistake him for a harmless drunk. Actually he is a terrorist or murderer with a dagger in his hand. In this case, the correct behavior would have been to sound the alarm and trigger your "fight or flight" stress mechanism. There is imminent physical danger and you either need to disarm him or flee the scene to survive. This is why it is important to sharpen your observational skills and evaluate your daily problems as to whether they are really dangerous or non-dangerous.

> About ninety percent of our daily confrontations in life are with imaginary predators, like those I conjured up during my first night in my tent on safari. We "stew in our own juices" and do battle with ourselves because the appropriate response to most of our daily encounters is neither to fight or take flight. Since there is nowhere to run and no one we can hit, most of us are caught in an "invisible entrapment" which can lead to a host of stress-related disorders.

> *It is better to learn to adapt to and live with situations than to react in a state of alarm and resistance. Alarm and resistance as a lifestyle lead to early exhaustion. Emotionally upset individuals literally withdraw all of their energy reserves ahead of schedule and run out of life too soon.*

SAFARI OF LIFE GUIDEPOSTS FOR MANAGING STRESS:

• Peg yourself accurately on the "cheetah" versus "tortoise" scale. Don't glamorize the cheetah image. Tortoises live much longer than cheetahs and get where they want to go more often than cheetahs; even though it takes more time, it involves less effort. You don't have to be one or the other. Just understand your emotional inclinations.

• If you're a type A, understand the risks. Get into the habit of listening to soft music and taking a relaxing time out before making the transition from work to home life.

• Most emotional reactions are automatic. Recognize when you are stressed and do some gross physical impact exercise by jogging, fast walking, or rebounding on a mini trampoline to re-balance your endocrine system.

• Examine your sense of humor to determine how it has served you. Is it mainly a warehouse for jokes and anecdotes, or does it function—as it should—to help you perceive your own occasionally ludicrous aspects? Laughter is contagious. Infect yourself and others with good reasons to laugh more.

• View change as normal. Constantly monitor and evaluate your capacity for change of pace, for flexibility, for new ideas, for surprises. Make some new friends and sample some new environments.

• There is no such thing as winning an argument. There is only winning an agreement.

• Don't engage in "all or nothing" management. If things don't work out exactly the way you had planned them, salvage a good situation. Don't be like the number one team that loses one game and thinks the entire season was a total failure. Don't look for unrealistic perfection in others or yourself. It will cause you to discredit your performance continually, and whatever you do will rarely measure up.

• Learn to say "no" as if it means "yes, I am already committed." One of the best ways to relieve stress is to schedule your time so that you can, comfortably, keep the commitments you make. Being "under the gun" all the time is characteristic of Type A behavior (which I refer to as "the frustrated cheetah"). It increases the risk of coronary and other stress-related diseases. Saying "no" in advance is much less painful than admitting "I'm sorry I couldn't deliver" later on. Only you can place yourself under the gun.

• Simplify your life. Get rid of the clutter and non-productive activities. Continue to ask yourself, at least once per week, "Beyond the normal routine of my daily work and schedule, what is this activity doing to further my goals and enrich my life?"

• Anger is one letter short of danger. Other than life or death situations, or when someone is being brutally victimized, there is no place in your life for anger. It is an emotion mostly reserved for spoiled brats or prejudiced ignoramuses. Find a relaxation technique even as simple as breathing slowly and deeply, counting to one hundred, or physically leaving the scene before you have time for an outburst that will benefit no one.

• Change lanes when the car behind you tailgates or drives close with its headlights on high beam. Never play tag with strangers on the highway for any reason. Your car is not a weapon. It is a transportation vehicle that needs to get you and loved ones to your destination safely.

3. Treat others the way they need to be treated to feel good about themselves. Collect their goodwill and appreciation. The absence of hate and the presence of love and acceptance seem to inspire the right kind of energy, or "eustress", as Dr. Hans Selye would call it. Eustress links the Greek prefix for *good* with stress in a similar way to *euphoria* and *euphonia*. The more we modify our self-centeredness and built-in selfishness, the more other people will accept us. The more acceptance we have from others, the safer we feel and the less negative stress we have to endure.

I defy you to spend a week to ten days at the Cottars 1920s safari camp on the Maasai Mara and come away feeling that you are the center of the universe. I am convinced you will remove any mask of conceit or selfishness you may be wearing and will come to terms with the fact that you are a member of the orchestra, including all the Maasai and wildlife living there. It continues to be one of the most enriching, energizing and yet humbling experiences I have ever enjoyed, which is why I return year after year.

Dr. Selye would have loved our safari because he observed that one of the most effective keys to successful living is to persuade others to share our natural desire for our own well-being. He would have enjoyed seeing how all the grazing animals on the Mara and the Maasai people live synergistically in harmony with one another to survive and thrive. Dr. Selye rephrased the biblical quote: "Love thy neighbor as thyself," into his own personal code of behavior, a code I try to practice every day and night, with everyone I meet:

> *"Earn your neighbor's love."*

Rather than trying to accumulate money or power, we would be better off acquiring good will by doing something that helps our neighbor, which includes all living things in every corner of the globe. "Hoard goodwill," Dr. Selye advised, "and your house will be a storehouse of happiness."

TAKING CONTROL OF CHOICES

Responding effectively to daily surprises and challenges is important. Just as important, in becoming a safari guide instead of a tourist on life's journey, is taking responsibility for our actions and choices, so the outcomes will be rewarding to ourselves and others. I believe our true rewards in life will depend on the quality and amount of contribution we make. From the Scriptures, to science, to psychology, to business, the documentation is the same: "As we sow, we reap." "You shall know them by their works." "You get out what you put in." "For every action, there is an equal and opposite reaction." "You get what you pay for." "Life is an unfailing boomerang. What you throw out goes full circle." The way we can build self-reliance is to recognize the number of alternative choices we have in a free society. When I interviewed our returning POWs and hostages, the thing they missed most was their "freedom of choice."

There are two primary choices in our lives: to accept conditions as they exist or to assume the responsibility for changing them. The price of success includes taking responsibility for giving up bad habits and invalid assumptions; setting a worthy example in our own lives; leading ourselves and others down a new and unfamiliar path; working more to reach a goal and being willing to delay gratification along the way; distancing ourselves from a peer group that isn't helping us succeed and therefore tends or wants to hold us back; and being willing to face criticism and jealousy from people who would like to keep us stuck in place with them.

My thirty years of research have convinced me that the happiest, best-adjusted individuals in their present and older lives are those who believe they have a strong measure of control over their lives. They seem to choose more appropriate responses to what occurs and to stand up to inevitable changes with less apprehension. They learn from their past mistakes rather than replay them. They spend time "doing" in the present rather than fearing what may happen.

Earlier I mentioned that to build our own self-reliance we need to replace fear with knowledge and action. The results of a University of Michigan study conducted some years ago have helped me reduce the part that fear plays in my life. The study determined that 60 percent of our fears are totally unwarranted, 20 percent have already become past activities and are completely out of our control, and another 10 percent are so petty that they don't make any difference at all. Of the remaining 10 percent of our fears, only 4 to 5 percent are real and justifiable fears. And even of those, we couldn't do anything about half of them. The final half, or 2 percent of our fears which are real, we can solve easily if we stop stewing and start doing…Knowledge and action.

Here is a formula. It seems simplistic on the surface, but has some real merit when you try it. There are 365 days in a year. Of all the fears that you now feel, or will ever feel, only 2 percent of them are a legitimate cause for concern and attention. Why not nip them in the bud early? Since 2 percent of your days in a year are "fear" days, you will be legitimately worrying about 7 days per year. Since most of us take about three weeks' vacation every year from our daily routine (and our fear), this gives us forty-nine weeks to absorb seven days of fear.

MY GUIDEPOSTS FOR FEAR-BUSTING:

Since only 2 percent of our fears are worth dealing with, I reserve

2 percent of my year—about seven days—not for fear, but for follow-through. I use the seven days to deliberately concern myself with what might go wrong during the year and then follow through to make sure it doesn't. That way I can enjoy the other 358 days because I have made a special effort to make them go right.

Usually, I manage to set aside an entire *F* day to slay my dragons. On that one day, every seven or eight weeks, I identify all the sources of current and potential worry and anxiety that might come my way. I write down my concerns and list some alternative choices I might have in dealing with them.

I also use the big red *F* days that I have put on my printed calendar, and in my hand-held electronic organizer, to focus on one major area of my life. For example, I pick one full day to devote to *Fitness Follow-through*. I schedule my annual physical exam, which includes an EKG stress test, heart and arterial body scan, blood work, and vision and hearing tests. I also make sure my regular six-month dental hygiene and examination appointment is set. Also, on that day, I give special attention to my nutrition and eating habits, and review my exercise regimen. Does that mean that I don't think about health and wellness on the other days? Of course not. Think of the single day like income tax day or election day, where your total focus is being aware of action you are scheduling and going to take.

Another bid red *F* day is for ***Family Follow-through***. Instead of worrying about not spending enough time on the family's needs, I use one full day to call and/or e-mail each member, wherever they are, and inquire as to how I can help improve the quality of their lives. I listen to their worries and concerns with empathy. Certainly every day is family day for most of us, but on ***Family Follow-through*** day, we make a special effort to be honest and open with one another. We set goals and priorities we never would set otherwise. Some of our most enjoyable family outings and events have been planned during these discussions. My decision to take my two sons on the next safari to Kenya happened on that *F* day.

Some other big red *F* days include **Finance, Friends, Future, Fun, and Facilities.** On *Facilities Follow-through* day, I review the conditions of my house, office and cabin cruiser. Our local maintenance crew look forward to that day because they usually get a lot of business prompted by my careful inspection.

As a result of these *F* days every seven or eight weeks, I keep up with handling major areas of responsibility and concern. I give them special periodic attention, and I take positive steps to minimize their impact. Having seven special days each year helps keep me in my usual state, which my friends describe as easygoing, mild tempered and relaxed. Because I follow through seven or eight times a year to keep potential fears from materializing, I can think of very few things that really frighten me, that is, except things with shaggy manes weighing four hundred pounds, with huge, sharp teeth, that hide in the tall grass, roaring just outside my tent at night. Maybe I need one more *F* day on my calendar, *Fangs* day, and I can spend the entire day on a hike with Calvin Cottar on the Mara, learning more about lion and leopard behavior, and how to follow through effectively if I ever find myself without an experienced guide by my side.

We are not only self-incarcerated victims of our own fears; we are victims of habit and group conformity. In a very real sense, each of us becomes a hostage of hundreds of restrictions of our own making. As children, we either accepted or rejected the environmental "uniforms" handed us by our parents. As teenagers and young adults, some of us had a strong need to conform to the standards of our peers. While we fooled ourselves into thinking we were being "different," we actually were as regimented as any army calling cadence and marching in full-dress uniform.

> To be self-reliant adults, we need to set some guidelines:
> Be different, if it means higher personal and professional standards of behavior
> Be different, if it means treating animals like people, and people as brothers and sisters
> Be different, if it means being cleaner, neater and better groomed than the group

> *Be different, if it means giving more in service than you*
> *expect to receive in payment*
> *Be different, if it means to take the calculated risk*
> *Be different, if it means to observe, listen and understand*
> *before passing judgment*

WHO'S IN CHARGE?

In my travels throughout the world, I see a concerning increase in the numbers of parents whose children rule the family. On airplanes and in public places parents seem to need to constantly bribe their kids with sweets and treats to keep them in check. It's as if children in our modern world have been coached by the ACLU to sue their parents for their rights, without any need for responsibilities. When I told John, our Maasai guide, that I was impressed by the fact that the Maasai infants and toddlers in the village we visited did not seem to whine and cry very much, he asked why that seemed unusual. When he visited California, he was puzzled by the fact that there were as many toddlers fussing as there were those who seemed to be enjoying themselves. I told him that in our child-centered homes, we indulge our children and try to purchase their affection to make up for our lack of quality time spent with them. He commented that the more we do for our children, it would seem to him that the less they are able to do for themselves later. The dependent child of today is destined to become the dependent parent of tomorrow, much more likely to see himself or herself as a victim of the system.

I told John I would like to see a Statue of Responsibility erected on Alcatraz Island in San Francisco Harbor to match the Statue of Liberty in New York. I have been lecturing and writing about the inscription I would like to see at its base if it's ever built:

"If you take good things for granted, you must earn them again. For every right that you cherish, you have a duty which you must fulfill. For every hope that you entertain, you have a task you must perform. For every privilege you would preserve, you must sacrifice a comfort. Freedom will always carry a price of individual responsibility and the just rewards of your own choices."

If it is built, I hope it's because we remembered freedom's obligations before it becomes too late. The shame would be if the monument was built for reminding us, after we fell off our pedestal as a great nation, of the forgotten lessons from our immigrant ancestors. John said he also hoped that Africa would remember its obligations to its animal and tribal ancestors as well, before it becomes too late.

My kids asked me to lighten up a bit in the passenger seat of the Land Rover as John was driving us to visit another pride of lions, so I told John a true story about a young couple who invited me to their home for dinner. This man and woman, both highly intelligent, with advanced college degrees, had opted for a "child-centered" home so their five-year-old son, Bradford (later I referred to him as "Bradford the Barbarian") would have everything at his disposal to be successful later in life in the competitive world.

When I arrived at their driveway in front of their fashionable two-story Tudor home, I stepped on his Spiderman doll getting out of the car and was greeted by, "Watch where you're walking or you'll have to buy me a new one!" Entering the front door, I instantly discovered that this was Bradford's place, not his parents. The furnishings, it appeared, were originally of fine quality. I thought I recognized an Ethan Allen piece that suffered from the final battle for Middle Earth in the *Lord of the Rings*. We attempted to have a glass of wine in the family room, but Bradford was busy ruining his new Game Boy unit. Trying to find a place to sit down was like hopping on one foot through a mine field, blindfolded.

Bradford got to eat first, sitting with us while we had our drinks, so he wouldn't be lonely. I nearly dropped my Merlot in my lap in surprise when they brought out a high chair that was designed like an aircraft ejection seat with four legs and straps. (I secretly visualized a skyrocket strapped under the seat with a two-second fuse.) He was five years old, and had to be strapped in a high chair to get through one meal!

As we started on our salads in the adjoining open dining room alcove, young Bradford dumped his dinner on the carpet and proceeded to pour his milk on top of it to ensure that the peas and carrots would go deep into the shag fibers. His mother entreated, "Brad, honey, don't do that. Mommy wants you to grow up strong and healthy like Daddy. I'll get you some more dinner while Daddy cleans it up."

While they were occupied with their chores, Bradford unfastened his seat belt, scrambled down from his perch, and joined me in the dining room, helping himself to my olives. "I think you should wait for your own dinner," I said politely, removing his hand from my salad bowl. He swung his leg up to kick me in the knee, but my old ex-Navy-jet pilot reflexes didn't fail me and I crossed my legs so quickly that he missed, came off his feet, and came down hard on the floor on the seat of his pants. You'd have thought he was at the dentist's office being drilled on with no pain killer. He screamed and ran to his mother, sobbing, "He hit me!" When his parents asked what happened, I calmly informed them that he had fallen accidentally and that, besides, "I'd never hit the head of a household!"

(Hearing me relate that, John was laughing so hard in disbelief, that he nearly veered into a herd of wildebeests). I finished this honest-to-goodness true account by saying that I knew it was time to be on my way when they put Bradford to bed by putting cookies on the stairs as

enticers. And he ate his way up to bed. "How are you ever going to moti-
vate him to go to school?" I asked quietly. "Oh, I'm sure we'll come up
with something," they laughed. "Yes, but what if the neighborhood dogs
eat what you put out? He'll lose his way just like Hansel and Gretel!"
They didn't even offer me dessert and I asked God for forgiveness for
not remaining silent as I drove back to the airport. When we got back
to camp, I wrote part of this chapter about life being as much a game of
choice, as it is a game of chance maybe even moreso.

Although many things in life are beyond anyone's control, you
do have a great deal of control—more than most of us are willing to
acknowledge—over many circumstances and conditions. To be different
and become a safari guide instead of a tourist, here are a dozen of the
most important guideposts:

*1. You can control what you do with most of your free time
during the day and evening.* Instead of watching other people making money enjoying their professions on prime time TV, turn off the TV
and start living in prime time. Read, interact with family, go out to ethnic
restaurants, attend artistic and artisan shows. Get up from the chair, and
explore the great outdoors.

*2. You can control how much energy you exert and effort
you give to each task you undertake.* Prioritize your projects.
Balance personal and professional goals. Finish what you start. Learn

what times of day your energy levels are the highest. Do important work during those peak periods.

3. You can control your thoughts and imagination, and channel them. Limit your TV news viewing to events immediately impacting your personal and professional life. Avoid violent entertainment. Read more inspirational biographies of people who have overcome enormous obstacles to become successful.

4. You can control your attitude. Hang out and network with optimists on a regular basis.

5. You can control your tongue. You can choose to remain silent or choose to speak. If you choose to speak, you can choose your words, body language and tone of voice. When you meet someone new, ask more questions and don't try to impress him or her with your exploits. The less you try to impress, the more impressive you will be. Say to yourself, "I'll make them glad they talked to me." And hope that they will be thinking, "I like me best when I'm with him or her."

6. You can control your choice of role models. The best role model is opposite to a celebrity in the sense that he or she is someone you can get to know personally and closely—preferably someone with a background or career path similar to yours; someone who has been where you are now. This is not to suggest that authors, teachers and leaders can't also be role models or mentors. A great deal can be learned from people whose ideas are available in print, audio, video and/or computer and web-based programs. If you encounter authors or speakers who seem to speak directly to *you*, don't just admire them; really learn from them by studying their work and their lives. Still, it's hard for that kind of role model to serve the full purpose, for which you should choose someone with whom you can spend time with personally (or via phone or e-mail) trading experiences and exploring ideas in direct conversation.

For personal role models and mentors, seek those who have not only achieved external success but whose whole lives, including their personal conduct, merit emulation. Career success can rarely be separated from character; one facet of a person's life invariably affects the other facets.

If you're young and relatively inexperienced, your best choices will probably lie among more mature, seasoned entrepreneurs. The combination of youthful desire and rich, seasoned experience can be very powerful. Rookies who are inclined by nature to be more enthusiastic and excited, often lack patience and sometimes staying power—but they also tend to be more innovative and less set in their ways. As they profit from veterans' stores of practical knowledge, the veterans can profit from youthful openness—not yet narrowed by frustration and defeat—to new ideas.

7. You can control your commitments, the things you absolutely promise yourself and others that you'll do. Don't over commit; in that way you won't have to make excuses when deadlines are

159

missed. Break your commitments into stair-step priorities and goals, ones that are reasonably easy to hit and easy to correct if missed.

8. *You can control the causes to which you give your time and emotion.* Focus more on positive programs with socially redeeming benefits. Instead of a protestor, become a producer and protector.

9. *You can control your memberships.* Congregate with people having similar goals or those who are overcoming similar challenges with knowledge, attitude, skills and habits.

10. *Fate is partly the hand you're dealt. You can't control that, but you can control how you play your cards.*

11. *You can control your concerns and worries.* We've discussed how you can deal more effectively with stress and fear. Find a relaxation and exercise program that helps you release tension. A quiet place, a garden, the sea, and soft music can do wonders for the soul. So can interaction with wildlife, as well as interaction with domestic animals. There is much comfort in the innocent loyalty of a dog and the independent yet cuddly curiousity of a cat.

12. *You can control your response to difficult times and people.* One of the best ways to overcome depression is to become active in helping other people in need. When I am down I visit the burn and cancer wards at the Children's Hospital, a senior citizen center, an orphanage or volunteer for some worthy youth group project. When dealing with difficult people, I spend the minimum amount of time possible with them and I attempt to determine if their "being difficult" is based on a temporary crisis or is ingrained in their personality.

If "difficulty" is their middle name, I relax and accept the fact that they are not going to change, no matter what I say or do, and I remain courteous and even-tempered and counter their negativity with quiet cheerfulness, which I must admit is "method acting." In studying actors like Meryl Streep and Dustin Hoffman, I have learned that the parts they are playing impact the biological processes inside their bodies.

> *Do we sing because we are happy, or are we happy because we sing? Yes, both statements are true. Happiness manifests itself in song, and the lyrics and tune that we choose to sing each day release the endorphins that give us a natural high, just as positive physical activity does.*

PRACTICE MAKES PERMANENT

Earlier in that day's game drive, we spent over two hours observing the female lions in the pride teaching the young cubs some lessons in stalking, ambush, and surprise. Although many of the survival skills of wildlife on the Maasai Mara are instinctive, such as the newborn wildebeest running at full speed with the migrating herd within 6 to 8 minutes of its birth, most of the lions' hunting skills are learned by observation, imitation and repetition.

Even as predators in training, those lion cubs were cuter than a big basket full of kittens playing with a ball of yarn, or a pet shop window full of golden retriever puppies playing with a rubber bone. To gain strength and agility they leaped on each other and tumbled over termite mounds and through the bushes pretending to do battle with each other. It was obvious, however, that on this late afternoon they were being instructed on how to stalk a wildebeest. John had pointed out that a full-grown male had strayed unwittingly away from the herd, and was grazing unaware in a dry river bed just below the lions' lair.

The older lionesses summoned the cubs, who followed behind the hunting party, far enough in the rear not to signal an alarm or get in the way. As the lionesses crawled on their bellies through the tall, savanna grass above the unsuspecting wildebeest, the cubs mimicked their actions. Just as if they were in a classroom, with a teacher who demanded complete quiet and total attention to her lecture, the cubs attention shifted back and forth from the huntresses to the hunted. When the kill was finally made, the lionesses did not begin feeding, nor did they damage the prey in any way, after the quick suffocation upon bringing the wildebeest down. The lionesses called the cubs to the prey, and then they lay under a tree to observe their offspring interact with the dead wildebeest. The young cubs pretended the gnu was still alive and simulated a surprise attack and jumped on the wildebeest's hindquarters and neck, as they had seen their mothers and aunts do.

After about a half hour of this practice-play, the cubs grew restless and began to voice their frustration in not being able to penetrate the wildebeest's tough hide with their claws or teeth. Whining to the older females, the cubs ran back and forth between the lionesses and the prey giving more than subtle hints that they were hungry and wanted their guardians to prepare the evening meal. The lionesses finally gave in to the youngsters' begging and they all dined together.

Man, of course, is the ultimate predator, able to reason, but more often rationalize his often irrational and aberrant behavior. As territorial as any lion, with instincts and cunning intelligence, man has one frightening character trait that is rarely seen among any other living species: mindful vengeance and violence for sheer emotional satisfaction. While our brains receive thousands of positive inputs daily, something inherent in our nature makes most of us lock on more strongly to the negative ones. And those negative ones not only abound, they're *pushed*, and not only by the underworld.

If you're still uncertain about the impact of commercial media on your life, here's what the Children's Workshop concluded after substantial research: "If Madison Avenue believes it can teach children on Saturday morning to buy a certain brand of cereal, why are we so complacent about the anti-social messages? You know the statistics. By high school graduation day, the average American student has seen 18,000 murders during 22,000 hours watching television – which happens to be twice as long as the time he or she spent in both grade school and high school. Television violence is dismayingly pervasive – and television of almost any kind offers only sensory stimulation.

Don't let network and motion picture executives fool you. It's not their First Amendment rights they're worried about, it's their wallets. They know that violence and shock content sells. Like drug peddlers might say in their own defense: "We're only giving them what they want." A task force on television and society appointed by the American Psychological Association found that the influence on views' attitudes and concepts in the same whether the television characters watched are real or fictional. I think secondhand violence and secondhand pornography are as damaging as secondhand smoke. If you're exposed, you're affected.

> *Observation, imitation, repetition, and internalization equals habit.*

But the good news is that you can change your life by changing your habits. Here are some guidepost rules regarding change:

Rule 1: No one can change you and you can't really change anyone else. You must admit your need, stop denying your problem, and accept responsibility for changing yourself.

Rule 2: Habits aren't broken, but replaced—by layering new behavior patterns on top of the old ones. This usually takes at least a year or two. Forget the 30-day wonder cures. I don't know where motivational speakers got the idea that it takes twenty-one days to gain a new habit. It may take that long to remember the motions of a new skill, but after many years of being you, it takes far longer to settle into a new habit pattern and stay there. Habits are like submarines. They run silent and deep. They also are like comfortable beds, in that they're easy to get into, but difficult to get out of. So don't expect immediate, amazing results. Give your skills' training a year and stick with it, knowing that your new ways can last a lifetime.

> Rule 3: A daily routine adhered to over time will become second nature, riding a bicycle. Negative behavior leads to a losing lifestyle, positive behavior to a winning lifestyle. Practice makes permanent in both cases.

This point is so obvious that it's often completely overlooked. If you do it right in drill, you'll do it right in life. Practice your mistakes on the driving range and you'll remain a high handicap golfer-duffer. Practice the correct swing for each club as demonstrated by a professional, and you may become a tournament player.

As a volunteer rehabilitation coordinator for returning air force and navy POW pilots from their prison camps after the Vietnam war, I had the first-hand experience of learning about some of the most remarkable mental accomplishments I've ever known. As a former navy pilot, and seminar trainer for Apollo astronauts, I already was familiar with the importance of mental and hands-on practice.

Did you hear or read in detail about the prisoners' habit patterns and practice sessions during their three to seven years of deprivation and boredom? In today's society, we can't even comprehend the stress involved in the stories of POWs in Iraq, who were detained for a week. What would you do if you were locked away for years, with no end in sight? Sleep? Read? Get depressed a lot? Feel sorry for yourself? Resent the folks back home? Go insane? Or would you, as many of them did, make a prisoner of war camp a self-improvement retreat? Several of our POWs made guitars out of wooden sticks and strings. Although their crude instruments made no sound at all, those who knew how to play practiced from memory, listening in their imaginations. They taught each other many new chords, finger positions and songs. Some who had never held a guitar before are now accomplished guitarists. Seven years is a long practice session!

Other POWs at the Hanoi Hilton fashioned piano keyboards by taking a flat board and pencil and sketching the keys to their actual size. Although their "Steinways" were silent and unplayable, they practiced day after day songs like "Clair de Lune" and enjoyed their favorite selections. There were no Bibles at the Hanoi Hilton, so the POWs pooled their memory banks and reconstructed hundreds of the most significant passages for their Sunday worship service. They communicated by a special type of Morse code by tapping on pipes between their cells. They taught each other skills from memory, discussed boyhood experiences of mutual interest and value, created complete mental diaries while in solitary confinement, invented hundreds of money-making ideas, and — perhaps most importantly—gained perspective by remembering and sharing the great ideals that are the foundation of their country's greatness.

I'm certain that Col. F. Spencer Chapman, who wrote *The Jungle is Neutral* about his own four-year ordeal behind enemy lines in the Malay jungle, nearly thirty years previously in World War II would have identified with our heroic Vietnam POWs. One dramatic story I have related during the past twenty years in my keynote speeches and seminars is the true saga of Air Force Colonel George Hall.

While in solitary confinement, he played an imaginary round of golf each day for five and one-half years as a POW in North Vietnam. He recognized that we have two choices in life: either play back haunting memories of fears, creating neurotic ideas of death, disease, confinement, fear and hopelessness; or play back winning experiences from the past and previews of coming "Oscar-winning attractions."

In his black pajamas and bare feet, in his solitary cube, Col. Hall played a round of golf every day for five and one-half years. He put every *Titleist 1* ball between the blue tees. He hit his drives, straight and true, down the middle of a plush, green fairway, sometimes that of his home club back in Mississippi, and perhaps other times at Pebble Beach or Augusta National. In his imagination, he replayed every good game he's ever played before during those five and one-half years.

He replaced every divot; raked the sand trap after blasting out; chipped onto the green; fixed every ball mark on the green; pulled out the flag; got on one knee to see whether the putt would break toward the ocean or up the hill; sank his putt and walked on to the next tee, washing his ball in the ball wash of his imagination.

Those mental simulations paid off when he got back to the real thing. After seven years of not being able to play golf, after five and one-half years in solitary confinement, and less than one month after his release, he was back in form. Col. Hall played in the New Orleans Open, paired with the senior pro, Orville Moody. He shot a 76! Right on to his four-stroke handicap. The news media ran up after the round and said: "Wow, Col. Hall, congratulations! That was really what you call beginners' re-entry luck, right?" Col George Hall smiled and said, "Not really. I never three-putted a green in all my five and one-half years."

The Edge is gained by practicing within, when you're without. It's actually seeing yourself doing, within, when you are without. It is recalling and reliving those positive experiences from your past, and then dwelling on those successes rather than your failures. It is creating the synthetic experience that will create the future, like the astronauts, by taking the correct theoretical information or data from other winners who have gone before you and practicing it as if you had accomplished it yourself.

By learning from coaches, mentors and experts, we can move from tourists to guides in the savage paradise called life. By practicing what's right instead of what's wrong, we can replace unhealthy habits with effective habits.

> *Imagination plus simulation equals realization.*

Rule 4: Having changed a habit, stay away from the old, destructive environment. Most criminals find themselves back in prison because they return to their former neighborhoods and gangs when released or paroled.

Dieters who reach their desired weight usually slip back into their former eating patterns because the new ones haven't been imbedded long enough to make them stronger than the temptations. Meanwhile, they should steer clear of buffets!

To remain optimistic and successful, you must avoid neighborhoods and Internet chat groups of pessimists and quick-fix pushers. To remain successful in business, you need to be on a team of which each member takes responsibility for being a leader. Recognizing your good habits is also essential, but for the moment, let's continue with overcoming the bad. My own bad habits include scheduling too many activities to be effective in all of them. Disorganized filing—sometimes in my computer filing too—makes me waste precious time finding research material. And I still don't balance my work with enough recreation and physical exercise. (At least I go on safari every year and walk a lot in the rarified air of the Maasai Mara highlands!)

Several years ago, I allowed myself to become very over-commit-ted and began arriving late for appointments, meetings and social events. Friends and associates called me "Waitley Come Lately. Then I chose new goals and made new affirmations: "I'm an on-time person," "I always arrive on time for meetings, appointments and trips." "Because time is important to others, I respect and honor the commitments I make" After a year or two of practice, I became known as "First to the Gate Waitley." What I'd learned was to frame a goal statement that's the oppo-site of the bad habits I wanted to convert, then schedule activities in my planner that confirmed my goal. The new habit patterns followed.

THE HABITS OF EXCELLENCE

Psychologists have done scores of studies of how habits are formed. We can now track a habit from the time sensory nerves carry messages to our fertile brains from our organs for hearing, touching, seeing, tasting, and smelling. The brain uses this information to make decisions, then sends working orders through motor nerves to the body parts needed for action.

It should come as no surprise, then, that habits are formed after the body responds the same way twenty-five or thirty times to identical stimuli. But here's an interesting discovery. After a certain amount of rep-etition, the message from the sensory nerves jumps directly to the condi-tioned motor nerves without a conscious decision by the brain. So while a mere twenty-five or thirty repeats can form a habit, I'm happy to report that the same number is involved in developing good habits, depending on input, practice and supporting environment.

If twenty-five or thirty repeats can form a new habit, you may wonder why making it permanent requires at least a year of practice. The reason is that the old patterns remain underneath. If you slip back—even if you associate with them—a link immediately recalls and tries to reassert them.

Here are some action tips for habit formation:

1. Identify your bad habits. When, where and why did you learn and develop them? Are you unconsciously imitating peers or negative role models? Do you use them to cover fear or feelings of inadequacy—emotions that would cause you to seek (false) comfort in tension-relieving instead of goal-achieving activities?

2. Learn what triggers your bad habits. Identifying your unwanted patterns makes replacing them easier, beginning with the triggers—which are often stress, criticism, guilt, or feelings of rejection. Recall the situations that cause you the most frustration and tension and plan ways to avoid or reduce them.

3. List the benefits of a new habit that would replace the old. Self-esteem, improved health, longevity, enhanced relationships, more professional productivity and respect, better focus, accelerated promotion potential and financial security...each helps lead to your ultimate goal of lifelong improvement and growth.

4. Say farewell forever to excuses for mistakes and failures.

Accept your imperfection when an old habit begs for attention. Instead of "There I go again," say, "Next time I'll be strong enough to do what's right." Instead of thinking "I'm too tired," say, "I've got the energy to do this and more." Change "It's too late" to "As I get organized, I know I'll have time."

5. Visualize yourself in the new habit patterns of a positive new lifestyle.

It takes many simulations and repetitions to spin new cobwebs on top of your old cables. If you want to give up smoking, intentionally sit in nonsmoking areas and request nonsmoking hotel rooms. Imagine a smoke-free environment, with hands and teeth of normal, healthy color. Internalize the sensation of fresher breath, cleaner-smelling clothes, furnishings, and most importantly strong lungs and a steadier heart.

> *You deserve as much happiness and success as anyone. You're worth the price—which is knowledge, attitude, skills and habit training. You control your thoughts, and your thoughts control your habits. Always remember that practice makes permanent. Your mind can't distinguish a vividly repeated simulation from a real experience. It stores as fact whatever you rehearse. The software drives the hardware—which is true for POWs, lion cubs and safari guides.*

I closed my journal and put down my pen. My kerosene lantern had nearly gone dry. I had no idea how long I had been scribbling these words, alone in my tent. I had become used to the sound of the lions roaring, the zebras barking, the baboons shrieking and the wind buffeting the canvas. I fumbled for my watch which was stuffed between my socks in my duffle back. I realized how unimportant a timepiece was here on the Mara. Who cares what time it is? We get up at daylight and go back to our tents sometime after dark.

When I asked John Sampeke, our guide, when his birthday was, he said he honestly didn't know. He knew his approximate age, and that he was born in his Maasai village sometime after the second rain. I thought it curious how much emphasis we in Western culture place on the passing of time, and make a big deal about celebrating our birthdays each year.

I looked at my watch. It was ten minutes to midnight on August 24th. I fell asleep wondering why I was giving any thought to birthdays.

CHAPTER ELEVEN
THE BIRTHDAY SURPRISE

August 25th was our last safari day and night together. I welcomed the dawn with mixed feelings because I had become so emotionally involved with the Maasai Mara that the Cottars 1920s camp actually was like a new oasis, a second home I didn't want to leave.

Nevermind that I planned to return on an annual pilgrimage. That was a year into the future. Now was now and I didn't relish the thought of packing my duffle bag and heading back to the gridlock of Interstate 5 in Southern California at rush hour.

My gloom was quickly dissolved with the recollection that today was my daughter Dayna's birthday, the event that had inspired the whole East African safari idea in the first place. Had I not thought of this special birthday present for her, as the fulfillment of a promise I had made to her twenty-five years earlier, I never would have bid for this trip at the auction benefit sponsored by my graduate school.

I chuckled to myself, thinking back to her early childhood years, as I adjusted the kerosene lantern in my tent so I could shave my stubbled face without severing an artery or reshaping my nose. Dayna had been our nature child since her toddler days. Her bedroom was always resplendent with animals, and I don't mean the stuffed kind. It was a pet store in miniature.

Now—with two children of her own, who we knew would be eager to share our safari experience the following year—her extended family back home consisted of a variety of dogs, horses, cats, birds, bunnies and chickens. Try taking all those to a kennel or "pet hotel" when you take a vacation. If it ever rained for forty days and forty nights in succession, she could have helped Noah fill his Arc with a number of species to assist in replenishing the earth.

I wiped the shaving cream off my face and donned a fresh set of khakis, a short sleeved shirt, my safari "flack" jacket, clean sweat socks and walking boots. How fortunate we were that the Cottars' offered complimentary laundry service to guests, with fresh clothes laid out every morning, and an opportunity for a massage and swim every late afternoon upon returning from drives or hikes. As rugged as the days were, we were pampered like heads of state.

Adjusting my Crocodile Dundee outback hat, I examined the smooth, whisker-free face in the mirror, trying to decide if I looked more like a seasoned Michael Douglas or maybe Harrison Ford. Leaning forward to get a better angle from the lantern in the morning darkness, I turned quickly away, with a shrug, aware that a reality check had reflected my appearance as more akin to Leslie Neilsen, the comedy lead in *Naked Gun*, *Airplane* and *Scary Movie* flicks.

As I walked down the path from my tent leading to the breakfast area, I glanced furtively into the thick brush on the adjacent hills to ensure that I wasn't about to be greeted by the resident lioness returning from her hunt last night or the male leopard who lived nearby a little higher up the mountain. There's still a running debate I have with my family. I say I whistle because I'm happy. They say I whistle involuntarily for stress relief!

On our final game drive of the trip we elected to head back to the Mara River to view the amazing spectacle of the wildebeest crossing and stop for a picnic lunch near the water. As usual, our good luck continued unabated as an abundance of wildlife, familiar and unfamiliar, decided to allow us the privilege of cruising the savanna with them.

We particularly enjoyed playing hide and seek with a flock of ostriches. They win the "African Idol" grand prize for the most entertaining wildlife show on the plains, especially the love-struck males. I've seen a lot of peacocks strut their stuff and spread their plumes trying to impress the ladies, but you haven't really lived until you've had a front row seat at the "big bird" dating game finale.

There is no doubt that Mother Nature made a mistake in designing ostriches or was in an especially devilish mood that day. They look like mutant descendents of smaller, two-legged camels, with one hump, feathers, shaved legs and beaks; or like feathered raptors without tails from a Michael Crichton movie about the lost world.

How can I adequately describe the male courtship choreography? They begin with ballet moves out of Swan Lake and soon they lose it completely with freestyle hip-hop, salsa, Irish Riverdance steps and jitterbugging. Their encore involves swinging their long necks around like gyrating garden hoses gone berserk from the water pressure with no one holding on. Those videos taken by my sons-in-law will be a welcome change of pace from the incessant television news commentary back home so obsessed with graphic scenes of violence, but rarely images of courage, hope and humor.

Leaving the ostrich comedy store, we headed to the Mara River. In the Maa language—the tongue which is the common bond between the Maasai clans—the word Mara means "spotted." The open plains must have appeared like a spotted cheetah's fur to the early Maasai as they were viewing it from a mountain or incline, with its patches of acacia scrub and olive trees that speckled the savanna. The combination of the richness of the grasslands and the permanent presence of water supplied by the Mara River make the area the one place where huge concentrations of game can still be seen in abundance. Nowhere else are lions so numerous, and we often stopped along the way to spend time with the healthy prides, said to be the finest in Africa, sprawled in a shady spot under the canopy of a wild olive tree.

Reaching the river we once again witnessed a scene of utter confusion, where masses of wildebeests and zebras were milling around on both sides. The herds that had crossed earlier were now grazing in the long, golden grass of Paradise Plain and continuing their migration journey. But many hundreds stayed behind as if they had been coached that there was safety in numbers and therefore wanted to cross in the company of thousands instead of hundreds at a time. As we watched, the zebras seemed to get their nerve up first and plunged into the swirling, muddy waters as if it was their assignment to lead the battle charge ahead of the wildebeests.

It was so surreal that it seemed more like an epic movie than reality, as the deafening hoof beats kicked up a cloud of dust that nearly eclipsed the sun, and the wildebeests charged forward and leaped into the river. Many crashed into the rocks below in shallow water, while others landed on top of others fighting the strong currents in deeper pools. It was sheer pandemonium and chaos as many plunged off banks too steep for safe entry and where many others were carried downstream and drowned in the treacherous rapids.

On both sides of the river, on the banks, in the trees, and circling overhead, were an ever increasing gallery of vultures, like Roman spectators, gloating with downturned thumbs in a coliseum of clashing gladiators. The crocodiles were there reminding us of prison guards whose mission was to make sure as few prisoners as possible escaped their river arena.

It was so unnerving to be that close to the action that we were grateful to only stay a few minutes before spending what was left of the morning with more pleasing sightings of giraffe, elephants, baby hippos and even rhino. We only saw two black rhinos from a distance on that trip since there are only a handful remaining, as a result of the devastating effects of poaching for their highly desired and supposedly magical horns. Everything about rhinos as well as crocodiles is prehistoric. The rhinos' spiked horn, lizard-like eyelids, three-toed dinosaur-like footprints and wrinkled hides bear testimony to their six million years on the plains. It is sad to contemplate that the black rhino will be but a memory in the not too distant future.

John found the perfect location for our lunch break. Our picnic spread was in a tranquil setting under the shade of a picturesque grove of leafy, riverine trees. Since we had parked far upstream from the herd crossing area, the only sounds we heard were intermittent snorts and grunts of the hippos below as they resurfaced or jockeyed for a roomier lounging area

---

in the river. John was decked out in his best red toga, sandals, necklace and staff, looking very much like the distinguished Maasai junior elder that he was, in his other life.

> Reminiscent of a glorious safari era of nearly a century past, we relaxed, dined and napped on giant, embroidered throw pillows and blankets, around an elegant table cloth set with china and serving dishes filled with a variety of vegetable and fruit salads, pheasant, wild pig and lamb. Fresh whole fruit, cheese and pastries followed, which I washed down with a fragrant chardonnay. This was my kind of campout in the woods!

While John and I scouted the area for a likely route to take an afternoon stroll to burn off a few of the hundreds of calories we had just ingested, my two daughters went in the opposite direction to find a suitable wooded enclave to serve as a makeshift restroom. It is more challenging for women to answer nature's call in the wild than it is for men, since there are no porta-potties on the Mara.

Not long thereafter, we heard Debi's unmistakable, high-pitched scream, like an SOS breaking the calm. Instinctively, John picked up his rifle and sprinted in the direction of the distress call. Tom, Ladd and I followed, fearing the girls may have had a close encounter with a hippo or crocodile. Just as John arrived at the scene, my daughters stepped out from their hiding place in the bushes.

"Did my screams sound realistic?" Debi, the obvious instigator, laughed as I arrived out of breath. John's brief smile of relief soon morphed into a school master's frown.

He began the lecture: "Don't ever play tricks like that on safari. You could underestimate the potential danger. Hippos and crocs are fast and deadly. To the crocs you are prey. To the hippos, you're an intruder and a possible threat to their calves. The only time a scream is proper, is when the danger is real. You scared your father and husbands."

John had sensed it was a prank because this was his regular picnic spot at the top of a steep embankment, safe from the animals below. They couldn't have made it up the cliff without an elevator! John had reacted reflexively, even though he knew the danger was nonexistent unless the girls had deliberately jumped off the edge, which was solid and clearly exposed.

John flashed his inimitable smile again, as he put his arm around Debi and Dayna, "Now we won't believe you if you come across a snake or a lion next time! We'll just continue our nap or keep walking, judging that you're just playing some silly game again."

The girls agreed that their charade had not been a good idea and we dropped the subject. Or they thought we all had dropped the subject.

Although Debi was the perpetrator, I felt that Dayna was a silent, but willing, observer.

> "What manner of retaliation is called for?" I schemed. Then a plot began to materialize. With both daughters relaxing on the throw pillows, John and I took a little stroll and we discussed our plan. In addition to being wildebeest, zebra, hippo and crocodile territory, it was also elephant country.

Fully engaged in the practical joke we were developing, John found the perfect prop. He identified a cake-shaped mound of well-preserved, totally dried elephant droppings. Of course I was well acquainted with our country-western references to "road apples" and "buffalo chips," however "elephant cakes" were a first.

Before you become repulsed and close the book, let me explain. This unique token of the elephant's presence was probably a year old, had absolutely no odor and looked like a potter had formed the perfectly round layer cake out of clay. John carefully wrapped the bounty in a table cloth and placed it in the back of the Land Rover, along with the left-overs from the picnic. As I considered the evening ahead, the drive back seemed to take forever.

When we returned to camp, we told the girls' husbands of our plan, while the girls were taking their showers. John and I then met with the very competent, congenial and enthusiastic kitchen staff who were charged with the most important aspect of the ruse. They went above and beyond the call of duty.

> With artistic flair the dessert was fashioned, complete with ornate, sugar flower petal decorations and "Happy Birthday Dayna" gracing the thick, pink icing on top of a safari-size, lovely birthday cake. Adding the final touch of two concentric circles of white candles, the staff had created a baker's masterpiece, looking simply delicious.

Allow yourself to sit with us—in your imagination—at the grand hardwood dining room table set for 16—for the dual celebration: our final supper with the Cottars, plus a birthday party for the guest of honor. It was enchanting. A cool August evening, with a slow fire burning. Fine china, crystal and silver candelabras adding to the ambience. Bleu cheese soup; endive salad, with raspberry vinaigrette dressing; beef and guinea hen; garlic mashed potatoes and fresh asparagus; mushrooms; a choice of dry French white wine or Pinot Noir, or both. A royal banquet right out of *Condé Nast* magazine.

Louise and Calvin Cottar were, as always, the perfect hosts. All 12 guests, including us Americans and our newly acquired Japanese, Mexican, British and Australian friends felt more relaxed than a long standing weekly bridge club. We had shared a bonding experience that you don't have to talk much about. You just nod, smile at one another, and know.

The anticipated moment arrived. We all "oohed and aahed" as the cake was brought in on a silver tray, looking as if it had been delivered by the French Gourmet. We applauded and the "Happy Birthday" song resounded out over the savanna, with all eyes focused on my daughter, Dayna, as she blew out the candles.

Then she cut the cake. Or she attempted to cut it. Dayna added more pressure to the cake knife, first with a puzzled look, and then her glance caught mine and her pupils constricted almost imperceptibly, that is to everyone but me.

"Dad," she smiled, "just what kind of cake is this?"

"Why, it's carrot cake, your favorite," I feigned innocent sincerity.

"An unusual kind of carrot cake?" she inquired. And then answered her own question, "But carrots aren't grown here in the Kenya highlands, Dad."

"Well, I called it carrot cake because it has the coloring and texture of authentic carrot cake," I stammered unconvincingly.

"But I can barely cut through it. Is it stale?" she offered sweetly, but sarcastically.

"Yes, the ingredients are a bit seasoned. It's called an "elephant cake," I confessed.

"Elephant cake?" she exclaimed, examining the interior cut more closely. "Oh my gosh, she laughed incredulously, "is this what I think it is?"

"Yes, it was John's idea to harvest an "elephant cake" to get revenge on you and Debi, while you were napping on the throw pillows by the river," I offered.

"Yeah, blame it on John," she shook her head. "I should have known you'd do something bizarre and one step beyond, Dad. Will you ever grow up?"

> As we were served the "real" birthday cake, the staff had baked earlier that afternoon, a German chocolate decadence, Dayna and Debi exposed my own foolish immaturity to the Cottars, the guides and guests, forever destroying any shred of credibility I may have pretended to represent as a psychologist and non-fiction author.

I felt a slight reddish glow creep up my face as my own daughters told the dinner party that "I had always had an empty room in my attic" which was either a birth defect or the result of flying too high without oxygen in my Navy jet aircraft when my girls were babies. They said I had scared trick or treaters by answering our front door in a monster costume on Halloween and that I threw marbles on our roof to mimic the sounds of Santa's reindeer on Christmas Eve.

I felt Debi went too far by relating to the amused guests that—instead of telling inspiring bedtime stories to my children—I would casually mention that a black panther had escaped from the zoo and was seen in our neighborhood, and then I would surreptitiously turn off the light, and crawl around their bedroom floor, making panting, growling noises. They said that they, and especially the younger boys, would dive under their covers, half-giggling, half-screaming, wondering whether it was their strange dad or a real werewolf in their room.

John mentioned the incident at the river to the Cottars and the others, saying that now he understood why Debi had acted that way. She had been programmed by her father.

My daughters completed the sabotage job which especially fascinated my sons-in-law, Tom and Ladd. Up until that moment, they had actually believed I was a respected professional. Now it was clear to them that I needed professional help.

Dayna recounted the time I had taken all the kids on a long drive from San Diego to Anaheim, not long after Disneyland had officially opened. When they all jumped with excitement on seeing The Matterhorn through the car window, I had rained on their parade, telling them that all the cars in the parking lot belonged to construction workers and staff in training. Disappointed and pouting they reminded me that we sure took a lot of long weekend drives that I seemed to enjoy the most.

Dayna said I told them we would have lunch at the Disneyland Hotel, which was open, to make the seventy-mile drive worthwhile. I then had marched them through the lobby up to the mezzanine to board the monorail, and on to a fabulous day and evening at Disneyland. "We only faked being sad, Dad" Dayna concluded. "By then we were wise to you and knew we were going to Disneyland the moment we saw the Matterhorn mountain from the freeway."

"But," Debi chimed in, "we weren't so sure when you took us for a scenic flight in your airplane and secretly turned the gas off over the ocean!"

"That's enough story telling," I interrupted. "Our guests are bored and tired. Let's call it a night."

As a post script to the birthday story, I must interject that the following year we returned to the Cottars' 1920s Safari Camp, with Dayna's children Alexander and Alissa, to whom we have referred in another chapter. It also occurred on the date of Dayna's birthday, August 25th. Only this time there was only one cake, and it was a real birthday cake with no pun intended. There was a large family from Belgium sharing the festivities with us, who spoke mostly French, but did understand basic English.

When Dayna blew her candles out that year, and made a wish, my nine-year-old grand daughter, Alissa, blurted out with obvious anticipation, "Is this cake made of elephant dung too, Papa?"

I tried to explain to our Belgium friends that last year had been a practical joke party, but that this was a freshly baked, delicious cake and certainly they would enjoy a piece. They glanced at each other and graciously declined, saying that they were full and rather tired from the strenuous day. They took their leave, hoping that our family enjoyed the dessert and the rest of the evening.

But don't let me confuse you by jumping ahead a year. Let's stay back in the previous year's trip, our very first excursion to the Mara.

After dinner I sat outside enjoying a glass of properly aged port under the most incredible African sky gleaming with more stars that appeared twice as bright and big as any I'd ever have seen before. Dayna and Debi walked up to my chair and hugged me good night. "This has been the best of all, Dad. Thanks, love you." Debi whispered.

I told Dayna I would buy her any authentic birthday keepsake from the Cottar's collection that she chose. "I've already had the best birthday present I will ever receive with this safari," she said. "Goodnight Dad. I love you."

What a wondrous gift it is to be a parent and realize that you are a parent for your entire life, not simply as a shepherd to your flock while they are in your care, but always. The laughter and child-like humor had been refreshing and relaxing. But nothing could exceed the one, single emotion that flooded my senses. Love of family, the greatest joy of all.

I already knew that the most significant love I have observed is the love between a mother and her children; but I could not possibly imagine that a mother's feelings could be anymore intense and total than my own.

I slept peacefully that night, with a final thought — courtesy of Robert Browning—resting on my lips as I lay my head on my pillow after a perfect day: "God's in his heaven, all's right with the world."

CHAPTER TWELVE
ENLIGHTENMENT

My daughters, Debi and Dayna, didn't seem surprised when I announced that I was going to stay at the Cottars' camp for an additional day and night to reflect on the experience and work on my book project. They reluctantly packed their duffle bags and said some tearful goodbyes to John and the staff. Calvin Cottar was taking them back to the Keekorok airstrip for the first short leg in a very long journey back to our concrete reality and the humdrum of advanced civilization. My son-in- law, Tom Arnold, the consummate investment banker, said it was an unmatched turning point in his life. He was grateful that he and Dayna had agreed to return with me the following year, with my two grandchildren Alexander and Alissa. My other son-in-law, Dr. Ladd McNamara, the bright, intense physician, was wondering what kind of health project he could enlist in to bring him back to Kenya. He and my daughter, Debi, had been as smitten with this indescribable saga as the rest of us. We didn't need to say much more and simply hugged and waved. It seemed as if only minutes had passed since our first sighting of the cheetah family upon our arrival. What was it about this short week that was life altering?

Why was this one outing in a lifetime more significant than all the books, other trips, conversations, lectures and retreats combined? I was beginning to understand and I needed time alone to center my thoughts and emotions.

I sat very still on the veranda of my tent—aware of my own heart beat—admiring the vastness of the plains, listening to the sounds of the day steal silently away, as the birds winged to the safety of their nests, and the night creatures began to stir restlessly from their slumbers. In that moment, I imagined this Eden, this cradle of civilization as a lovely woman. It was the same feeling I had when I arrived, which is why I had the flashback to the film *Somewhere in Time*.

> The wind in the Kenya highlands, above the camp, had seemed to have whispered directly to me, as Mother Earth might have, were she a woman, "You have come home!" And I knew that whenever I heard the theme songs from "Out of Africa" or "Somewhere in Time"—always my favorites—I would imagine that the lovely, old woman—who whispered in Richard Collier's (Christopher Reeve's) ear, "Come back to me"—was actually here, in this magical place, urging me to return. And so I have, and so I will.

But why? Why here? Why not at my favorite boyhood haunts on the sands and coves of La Jolla, California before the crowds arrived? Why not at the Great Barrier Reef in Australia where I loved to spend my holidays? Or the beautiful south island of New Zealand, or the lush green glades in Ireland, or in the pristine Canadian or Colorado Rockies? Or in Lanai, Kauai or Polynesia? Or in any of the Holy cities? Or in the forests, near the rivers and lakes, and painted deserts? Or in the Alaskan wilderness? Or in Asia, where I travel often and sense the ancient giant awakening that will lead the future of human economic development?

As darkness fell softly like a velvet cloak all around me, I was greeted by the stars and planets overhead, appearing to me like a vast gallery of eager spectators sitting high up in the balcony to view the Maestro's symphony of life below. That was the word I was groping for. It was the word *life*.

Here I was connected to life more than in any other setting. This was a mirror into which you peer and see more than just your own face. In our Western culture, and in all industrialized societies, the mirror is like a shiny pool where Narcissus gazed vainly and constantly at his own reflecton. We are self-absorbed humans in the present, who believe the universe is centered around our individual aspirations and that wildlife are more like pets, pawns and servants, to meet our needs, wants and diversions as court jesters and cheetahs might have been to us, were we all Assyrian kings. There is wildlife, to be sure, in the other places I've mentioned. But nothing can match the diversity, sheer abundance and variety of life in East Africa. The pyramids of Egypt speak volumes about life existing over two thousand years ago. But the ancestors of the handful of black rhinos—our living dinosaurs in the Maasai Mara—have grazed here for six million years.

Here in East Africa, the past lives in the present; not merely in the form of fossils, artifacts and ruins. History is alive on the Maasai Mara in Kenya. The museum of natural history breathes and pulsates before your eyes in the greatest assembly of wildlife on earth. You don't need to press a button to activate an audio-visual display of how it was back then. You sit and watch, you smell and listen. You are connected.

Then and now are one in the same.

And you don't need to be an animal rights' activist or environmentalist to experience the awe of these magnificent surroundings. You can be a people person, conservationist, history buff, camera bug or an explorer and feel the same spiritual bonding, just as the Cottars and Leakeys have since the early 1900s. I'm certain you are familiar with the series of expeditions conducted first by Louis Leakey and his wife Mary, and continued later by Mary and son Richard Leakey. Among Louis Leakey's academic protégées were Dian Fossey, who you'll remember from her characterization by Sigourney Weaver—in the riveting film *Gorillas in the Mist*—portraying her courageous, but tragic life studying the mountain gorillas of Africa; and Jane Goodall, who became well known to the general public for her unique and revealing studies of the behavior of chimpanzees.

In 1972, Richard Leakey reported the discovery of a 1.8 million-year old skull of modern humans from Koobi Fora. Lying on the eastern shore of Lake Turkana in Kenya, Koobi Fora is one of the world's leading prehistoric sites for the study of early humans. In 1978 Mary Leakey found a trail of clearly defined, ancient hominid footprints of two adults and a child – approximately 3.5 million years old—imprinted and preserved in volcanic ash from a site in Tanzania called Laetoli.

On our walks and hikes, I, my children and grandchildren made our own footprints; however they would soon disappear after the first rain. The mindprints, however, will last for the rest of our lives. This land upon which we trod, so briefly, is only a fraction of that upon which the Maasai tribes and their ancestors have driven their cattle for countless thousands of years. They are indelible in a timeless African dream and have stubbornly attempted to keep their heritage intact, remaining visibly confident in their identity as a people. In truth, we were transient, bed-and-breakfast guests of those proud people, whose customs and traditions survive and endure, even though their society may not.

As I have written earlier, they are as much endangered species as the black rhino and their fate is inextricably woven into that of our own society. We in America are a very young and naïve culture, in spite of our inventiveness, entrepreneurship and technological genius. Unless we learn from the history of extinct civilizations that synergy is the key to survival, and that wisdom must accompany power, we could, ourselves, become but a comet in the universe, burning brightly but briefly. In my humble opinion, the survival of the fittest will give way to the survival of the wisest if this circle of life—our earth—is not to become a science project for future space travelers, like the planet Mars.

Being a card-carrying optimist, I prefer to see my glass as almost always full, rather than half-full or half-empty. I believe that we will catch the reflection of our own arrogance in the mirror and become stewards and shepherds of those whose lives are in such a precarious state of imbalance, along with our own. I can do little more than set a worthy example with my own actions in the hope that I can influence those who follow in my footsteps.

I am not into the polarity of politics, nor do I blame our government for our current state. I must defer to the Maasai definition of motivation: "When the belly's empty, you start to think!" Our major problems in my opinion, stem from our feelings of entitlement and our obsession with immediate sensual gratification. Our newly arrived immigrants are hungry for food and knowledge, and are willing to put in the study and effort to gain the KASH, the knowledge, attitude, skills and habits that have always been the ingredients for achievement and success. Those who have been born in America or who have enjoyed the benefits of abundance for a number of years, often begin to rest on past laurels and become apathetic and selfish. They lose their sense of wonder, their curiosity, their incentive to continue learning, their interest in the common good and look for someone other than themselves to take responsibility for their outcomes.

I spent the rest of the evening writing in my journal some of the lessons I had learned in this savage paradise and some of the ways in which I would manifest my learning as how I would live my life from this day forward. To say that I had been transformed is an understatement. More accurately, I had traded my former identity for a new one, complete with a new set of senses, to better see what before I never noticed; to better hear what I seldom listened to; to smell fragrances that before had only come from bottles, ovens and flower petals; to touch textures in the way a blind person would; and to feel in my heart, those half-forgotten vibrations of love and passion that transcend most human interactions. I decided to take time to really live.

TAKE TIME TO LIVE

Time never stops to rest, never hesitates, never looks forward or backward. Life's raw material spends itself *now,* in this moment—which is why how you spend your time is far more important than all the material possessions you may own or positions you may attain.

Positions change, possessions come and go, you can earn more money. You can renew your supply of many things, but like good health, that other most precious resource, time spent is gone forever. Each yesterday, and all of them together, are beyond your control. Literally all the money in the world can't undo or redo a single act you performed. You cannot erase a single word you said; can't add an "I love you," "I'm sorry," or "I forgive you"—not even a "thank you" you forgot to say.

Time is the only resource or gift distributed indiscriminately to everyone, at least by the day or week. Each human being in every hemisphere and time zone has precisely 168 hours a week to spend. Scientists and computer experts can speed up data transmission to perform millions of transactions a second, but they can't create a single new second.

None of us seems to have enough time, yet we all have all there is or ever will be. It would take a hundred lifetimes to accomplish all we're capable of, but we're given just one for learning and experiencing as much as we can, for doing our best. If we had more time, there would be less need for books like this one, less need to make plans and set priorities. If we had forever, we could probably wing it every day and still end with immense knowledge, possibly even wisdom. But we're strictly limited to those 168 hours—10,080 minutes—a week, which is why Benjamin Franklin urged us not to squander "the stuff life is made of."

One of life's great ironies is that time crawls when we're young and flies as we age. When we were children, the ride from the airport to Disneyworld lasted forever. It took an eternity for holidays and summer vacations to arrive—birthdays, too, until the twenty-first, which had always been far distant in the unimaginable future. Then, slowly at first, the clock began to accelerate. The thirtieth birthday seemed to arrive inexplicably soon after the twenty-fifth. The fortieth came altogether unexpectedly, and with less than a hearty welcome. The ten years between thirty and forty—a decade of watching children's rapid growth from toddlers to teens and of often arduous climbing of corporate ladders—passed like three or four.

After age forty, I began linking time to the seasons. There was a blur of time from winter skiing to spring cleaning and onto summer travels and fall commitments. I lived in short swallows of breath, climbing mountains, weathering unexpected storms, enjoying experience and growth and feeling that six months raced by like a week. After fifty, I realized from very personal experience that time appears to race with the years because we understand how precious and rare it is; we appreciate our remaining portion as if it were pure oxygen escaping from a beautiful balloon that can never be refilled.

Many people live in the past, wishing they could put the clock in reverse, largely to undo mistakes. Most people live in the future, wishing for and worrying about what they want to have and to do but can't—instead of enjoying what they have and doing what they can do, but don't. They put happiness and fulfillment on permanent layaway. We can't relive yesterday and mustn't waste today by living in a fantasy tomorrow. Only the actions we take here and now can create tomorrow's real promise. We will not have this day or moment to enjoy again.

When we were five years old, one year represented twenty percent of our total lives. At fifty, a year represents two percent, or one fiftieth, of our life experience. No wonder it took so long for holidays to arrive when we were in grammar school—and little wonder also that after age fifty, when a year represents such a small portion of the time we've already spent, it goes by in a seeming blink of an eye. It's a little like a videotape speeding up as it rewinds and accelerating almost wildly near the end of the reel. So goes your remaining time as it dwindles down.

Take time to hear a robin's song each morning
Take time to smell the roses as you go
Before you leave, please say "I love you
To the ones you know
Take time out for a sunset
And its afterglow

Take time to climb a tree with kids this summer
Explore each country back-road you can find
And take a moment now and then
To build a castle in the sand
Take time to hike that mountain
When you can

Take time to play, your work can live without you
Give up the urgent for the afternoon
And take a loved one by the hand
And slowly gaze at that full moon
Don't let this minute pass you
For the years go by too soon

And make each day "safari" day
Before this moment slips away

Take time to live.

No one can reasonably claim that the daily life choices are easy. I trust I'll never forget M. Scott Peck's great *The Road Less Traveled*—inspired by *The Road Not Taken*, a well-known poem by Robert Frost—whose opening line consists of three words: "Life is difficult." No doubt it has always been difficult in various ways, but some stretches are more difficult than others, and America has known far easier, happier periods. The increase in violence is frightening, not only via terrorism from outside our borders—but also that spawned in our own cities, suburbs, schools and streets, which betrays the underpinnings of our family life, our sense of responsibility, our culture.

Many of our children seem destined to live in a world of angry anarchy, with all that it means for society as a whole. We worry about our children, in this respect and others. Confusion grows, tempers are raw, relationships are strained, the traditional American optimism has been worn a little thin. Economic security—homeland security—security of all kinds seems to be disappearing. All of this is true, and most of it is rightfully worrying—but at the same time, the opportunities for personal growth and success are unparalleled.

As we grow older, we recognize that certain battles are no longer worth getting upset about. Therefore we should choose our conflicts carefully, just as we should choose the road on which we walk with increasing care. Which road is best? As Robert Frost said, the road less traveled made all the difference. If that's the road you've chosen—never mind whether you're racing ahead like a cheetah, struggling on an upgrade like a tortoise, or resting a moment while you catch your breath—you know that life is not a book that is finished when you've read its last pages.

Individuals on the road less traveled are generous to others because they have a strong sense of their own self-worth and don't need to hide behind impostors' masks. They can give freely of themselves without feeling depleted. They know the only thing they can really keep is what they're willing to give away. These travelers also know that they can never be certain of what lies around the next bend. So they walk in quiet faith, one step at a time, one day at a time, reaching out to one person at a time—starting with members of their own families, their neighbors, and their teammates at work.

Do you consider the quality of the journey as important as the result? Is your definition of success a million dollars in your bank account and a vault stuffed with stock certificates, or is success taking the high road and placing value on people and the precious, natural world—your family and others whose goals you can help reach?

If you could balance the demands of your business and personal life with more outside activities, what would you choose? To spend some weekly time reading to the elderly in a community retirement home? Take more walks on the beach or in a park? Come to Kenya on a safari? Volunteer for a drug awareness program for teenagers?

It's easy to be caught in a narrow, constricted perspective, easy to forget that life—like our money, property, jewelry, and antiques—is something we never really own. We've only been entrusted with our possessions, given the privilege of enjoying them for a few seasons, after which we must pass them on to the next caretaker. I will always remember that to the Maasai, land is God's property because it was created by God. How can you own something you are a part of? As a pastoral people, moving as nomads with their herds, the Maasai also saw themselves as caretakers, reasoning that since wildlife had always been free to migrate from millennia to millennia, why shouldn't they? They considered land as theirs to use, but never to own.

Whatever you *do* do, whatever your business is, whatever your professional or personal mission statement, ask yourself about your impact on others. Are you planting shade trees for future generations, under which—you yourself—may never sit? How do you find these roads less traveled? You can't find them in an atlas or in a travel agent's brochure. It's harder than that, but also easier. They are roads you build yourself, roads that lead into your own mind and essence. And one way or another, you must travel the road you yourself have designed.

The reality is that my time is dwindling. I've now lived much longer than I'll continue to live. All the more reason to keep searching for the road less traveled, keeping my priorities in line. I'm going to put more effort into enjoying the ripple effect that comes with making a difference. The ever wider concentric circles from a stone thrown into a pond is an appropriate analogy. Today is a good time to start making your own waves in your world. Your smallest, seemingly most insignificant action can be of great importance to a family member, friend, business associate, animal or stranger.

One simple truth can never be overemphasized: Success will not be based on your bank account or your earthly possessions. Your sense of fulfillment will always be in direct proportion to how wisely you use your time and how well you maintain your health, both of which will be gone forever once they are spent. Only by nurturing these twin components will your life be balanced, and in the process you will help smooth the ride on your safari to fulfillment.

I've made a little list of things I'll do more and less of from now on:

> Laugh at my misfortunes more and at other people's predicaments less. Spend more time counting my blessings, less time scrutinizing my blemishes.
>
> Spend more time playing with my children and grandchildren, less time watching professional athletes perform. More time enjoying what I have, less time thinking about the things I don't have.

Walk in the rain more without an umbrella and listen less to weather reports. Spend much more time outdoors in East Africa and much less time in tall buildings and big cities.

Eat more of everything healthy and delicious, less of everything each meal, saving enough on the bill to feed a starving child.

Do more listening and less talking so I can learn to understand rather than being desperate to be heard. Spend more time looking at trees and climbing them, less time flipping through magazines made from dead trees.

Get more beach sand between my toes and less friction between myself and others. Take more long baths and fewer showers. Spend more time with old people and animals, less time with strangers at clubs and parties.

Act the age of my children and grandchildren more and act my own age less. Give my loved ones more tender touches and much less advice.

> *Spend more time fully involved in the present moment, less time remembering and anticipating. Become more aware of my core values and life mission, and less concerned with the reasons why I might not measure up.*
>
> *Smile more, frown less. Express my feelings more, try less to impress my friends and neighbors.*
>
> *Forgive and ask forgiveness more, and curse my adversaries less—but most of all I'll be more spontaneous and active, less hesitant and fearful.*

When a great idea or spur-of-the-moment adventure pops up—a safari of any kind, an open house at school, a game of hide-and-seek, an opportunity to solve a problem at work or to satisfy a disgruntled customer, to understand someone who looks and believes differently than I do, to go on a hay ride, to be invited to build a snowman or paint over graffiti, to watch a lunar eclipse or a double rainbow—I'll be more inclined to jump up and say, "Yes, *let's do it!*"

I'm going to dedicate myself to live this new way every day. I'll never have all the moments I've missed, but I do have all the time remaining.

I put down my pen, took a sip of iced tea and watched the tall, effortless stride of John Sampeke as he came up to my tent from the tall grass in front of my veranda, rather than up the winding dirt path.

"I saw you through the binoculars on my walk through the bush, and wondered why you have been here at your tent all day," he seemed concerned. Are you not feeling well?"

"No, I couldn't be better, John, except that I'm not ready to leave in the morning?" I replied.

"What have you been writing in that diary, Denis?" he queried. "It must be important to keep you away from the wildlife."

"I'm trying to think of some way to finish this book, so that the reader can share a bit of what this connection with the past and present really means. Words are so inadequate." I showed him my little verse on *Take Time to Live.* He said he especially enjoyed the part about sunsets and full moons.

"Put your writing away and come with me," John said, as he checked his wrist watch. "It's five thirty in the afternoon. We have just enough time."

"Time for what?" I called after him, as he jogged toward the Land Rover. "Wait up, it's hard to keep up with you at this altitude," I complained.

"All the more reason you should come here every year, to get back in shape. You just barely survived our walk over that little hill the other day," he grinned.

"Little hill?" I pointed. "I ski down hills with less inclines than that!"

We joked and laughed as he drove out onto the Mara on that late afternoon, fifteen thousand miles from my home. It was our final drive before my trip to the airstrip early the next morning, and I wondered where we were going and why.

John shared with me many proverbs and fables that had been passed down through the centuries by the Maasai elders to the next generation. I had failed to consider that much of African history has been passed on by the spoken word, and only in relatively recent times, has this history been in written form.

"I liked your story about *The Jungle is Neutral*, Denis," John offered as we headed in an unfamiliar direction we had not visited with my family on previous drives. "I hope you include it in your book. It is so true that a guide is unafraid because of his knowledge and experience. And that the tourists, are frightened due to their lack of knowledge, skills and training. Even after a week, I noticed how totally comfortable your family members became, once they began to learn how to recognize what is really dangerous and what is life supporting," he reflected.

"Hey, John, you're becoming somewhat of an intellectual. If you're not careful, you won't want to wear your red toga anymore and will trade it in for an Armani suit and briefcase," I chided.

"Not to worry," he answered. "The price of one Armani suit would feed a Maasai village for three months!"

We then talked about what I considered some of the greatest wisdom I had gained while here and throughout my life, which interested him, since I had been wandering throughout the world for more than a quarter of a century longer than he had. I thought carefully and said that one of the greatest proverbs or wise sayings that I had ever learned and tried to emulate was contained in Reinhold Niebuhr's classic work *The Serenity Prayer*, which he authored in 1932 as the ending to a longer prayer:

> God grant me the Serenity,
> To accept the things I cannot change;
> The Courage to change the things I can;
> And the Wisdom to know the difference.

I told John that I had been teaching a stress management workshop in conjunction with "The Psychology of Winning Seminars" based upon those words—to some of America's most prominent corporations and to the general public—for over thirty years. As we neared our destination, I told him my interpretation:

Accept the Unchangeable—Everything that has already happened is history. It can be interpreted in many ways, but cannot be altered as an event. Serenity is achieved when you learn to convert failure into fertilizer, stumbling blocks into stepping stones, and misfortunes into learning experiences. There is no such thing as getting even or getting revenge. Vengeance is negative energy and doomed to result in despair and more failure. Succeeding, in the face of adversity and in spite of naysayers and detractors, is the only positive way to avenge wrongdoing or injustice. Certainly we need to defend ourselves in life threatening situations, but we must be very wise in knowing our adversaries and in measuring the impact of our actions and responses.

Change the Changeable—Our only control in the outcomes of our lives is in our response to what has happened, our anticipation of what will happen in the future, and our choices and decisions on a daily and minute-by-minute basis. This is why knowledge, attitudes, skills and habits need to be internalized from reliable mentors, role models and coaches, whose characters as well as professional attributes are worth emulating. We spend far too much time and energy hoping that others will change, when we ourselves must change what we do and what we don't do to influence others to follow our lead. True courage is based on being prepared and being flexible in the face of surprises.

Remove Yourself from the Unacceptable—Part of the process of being serene, wise and courageous is in knowing when to "fight, make a stand, or take flight." Being able to anticipate what is a dangerous situation and to avoid it is one definition of maturity and countenance. Wise individuals change itineraries, directions, locations, environments, plans, actions, behaviors, friends, role models, peer groups, choices and responses, based upon their assessment of whether the situation is dangerous or non-dangerous, productive or futile, and being able to distinguish patience, persistence, prejudice, ignorance and stubbornness from each other.

John agreed that The Serenity Prayer contained the basics of what he had learned as a Maasai warrior, junior elder and safari guide in Kenya's Maasai Mara. I recalled, as we got out of the Land Rover, that he had received the highest grades of any Maasai guide during his professional training. Why was I lecturing someone who was living what I was mostly preaching? I shook my head and followed him out into the middle of nowhere.

What a setting! No buildings, no people, no vehicles, no aircraft, no smog and no cacophony of noise. Total quiet except for an occasional zebra, wildebeest and bird of prey calling to one of its own. We had seen a few lions on our way, but they were still relaxing under olive trees. I don't suppose I'll ever get enough of lions, no matter how many times I return to their majestic land. The lions blend into the tall grass and become indistinguishable from it. The grass must have rain to nourish its growth. The plant growth, as a result of the rain, determines the number of herbivores it can sustain. They, in turn, regulate the number of predators that can survive. And so the cycles have repeated, along with the Great Migration, in the circle of life, since the beginning. Seed, sprout, bud, blossom and seed. Each of us a product of the earth and forever bound to it.

I couldn't figure out why John had taken me on a hour drive to the very middle of the Cottar's range in the Maasai Mara. I looked to the north, east, south and west. All I could see were blue-green mountains,

and the saffron glow of the plains rolling and stretching to infinity. No matter in which direction I would stare, there were no visible landmarks. I thought if I had started walking, I could have walked for years, without arriving at a place populated by people.

"Don't play a trick on me and ask me to find my way back to camp or to Nairobi, John!" I smiled. "I give up," I continued. "Obviously we're not here to spot and study wildlife."

At exactly 6:20 pm on that August afternoon, John had me perform what I thought was some kind of ancient Maasai ritual. He told me to stand facing true north with my eyes closed He then asked me to fully extend both arms from my sides, my left arm parallel to the ground pointing west; my right arm, fully extended, parallel to the ground, with my hand pointing east. He instructed me to turn my left arm so that my extended fingers were closed like a fin, with my left palm facing down; and had me turn my right arm so that the fully extended fingers on my right hand, close together like a fin, had my right palm facing up.

"Now open your eyes," John said quietly, "And slowly push your left palm down and, at the same time, slowly raise your right palm up."

You would have had to be there to believe it. Glancing to the west, I saw my left hand push the most enormous, molten melon ball of a sun down toward the distant horizon. Because there were no visual obstructions, inversions, and low cloud layers of any kind, and since the land seemed totally flat for hundreds of miles in each direction, the sun appeared to be magnified a hundred times. It was like the world's biggest hot air balloon, slowly settling as it cooled and touched the earth. I've seen many sunsets from mountain tops and on the ocean, but this magnificent spectacle took my breath away. I couldn't even say, "Wow!" I was speechless.

Just then I looked to the east as I raised my outstretched open palm from the horizon, and saw a sight I doubt that I'll ever live long enough to repeat. I held in the palm of my hand and raised slowly into the sky, the most gigantic, azure-yellow, full moon I have ever witnessed. I didn't know whether to look east or west, because I didn't want to miss a moment of this ethereal experience.

As I pushed the sun below the far western horizon, the olive and acacia trees began to cast ever lengthening shadows, and in the thickening dusk, the plains became like a leopard's or cheetah's coat, with alternating gold and dark spots and flecks as the trees and bushes became silhouettes and the colors changed, as if I were viewing it through a pastel-filled kaleidoscope, as wisps of high cirrus clouds reflected the sun's finishing touches to another day.

As I raised the perfect East African full iridescent moon above the earth, it, in turn, illuminated the eastern Mara with a totally different effect. It was sheer enchantment; what else can be said? I was hypnotized, moved beyond words. Spellbound.

I had come to Africa to fulfill a promise. I was to leave Africa connected to my own soul.

Throughout my life I have been counseled by wise men and women that we humans are unique because our souls live on beyond mortality. In this instant, I became aware that my soul can reveal its presence while I am living. It is that essence within us that gives us the capacity for experiencing overwhelming beauty through each of our senses, in every fiber of our being.

As a former military warrior, steeled to quench emotions, as I flew my Navy jet off carrier decks to defend my land against aggressors in years past, I found that either my seasoning or my poetic core had peeled away my armor, and I stood looking at my friend and guide, John, with liquid eyes as I bit my lip and said: "Thank, you buddy. You are like a brother."

John smiled and put his arm around my shoulder. "I love you too, my brother."

And so we are, have been, and will be. Present, past and future. Re-connected.

EPILOGUE
AN INVITATION

On my way to Africa again…with loved ones.

As you contemplate Creation
Wondering "why" and "who" you are;
And why life shines bright, but briefly
Like a cosmic falling star.

Bring your ponderings to Eden
To the place of mankind's birth;
Fuse the past into your presence
In the arms of Mother Earth.

Tell the lions of your struggles
Tell the elephants and birds;
Take communion here in silence
Midst the ever constant herds.

And relish in the knowledge
That "your being" fits this song;
That the harmony is real here
In this land where you belong.

Makes no difference your religion
For the Maestro welcomes all;
You'll be closer to your Savior
Than in any hallowed hall.

Hear the wind in the acacias
Whisper "welcome home dear friend;"
To the magic of beginnings
Where the story has no end.

When you're seeking self-fulfillment
In your urgent quest to win;
You can rest here, watch and listen
To the music deep within.

You'll find answers to your questions
You'll release the unknown fears;
Of what happens in the future
Far beyond your mortal years.

Truth oft times evades us
No matter how hard someone tries;
It arrives by revelation
Standing right before our eyes.

I thought myself a wise man
But a novice to be sure;
Who has just begun his journey
Into love that's true and pure.

I'm a living, breathing instrument
One of billions on the stage;
Who plays his part with passion
With some notes on history's page.

Come with me to Kenya
Leave your masks and stuff behind;
Travel light with no agenda
Just an eager, open mind.

You'll discover in the vastness
Your connections to the whole;
And find inner peace and beauty

...On Safari to Your Soul

ENDNOTES

[i] Saitoti, Tepilit Ole, *Maasai* (New York:Abrahams, 1980), p.25

[ii] Dov, Pereta, Elkins, *Glad to Be Me* (New York: Prentice-Hall, 1976), pp. 28, 29

[iii] Col. F. Spencer Chapman, *The Jungle is Neutral* (New York: W. W. Norton & Co. Inc., 1949)

[iv] KASH acronym created by Harold Hook, founder of the Modelnetics' communications system

[v] Rheinhold Neibuhr, The Serenity Prayer, New York, 1932

To order additional copies of

Safari to the Soul or other Denis Waitley products, please

Contact: 877-929-0434,

Email: service@deniswaitley.com or

Go To: www.deniswaitley.com

For more information about additional publications

and services of Denis Waitley contact:

Denis Waitley International

2835 Exchange Blvd., Ste 200

Southlake, Texas 76092

Phone: 1-877-929-0439

Email: info@deniswaitley.com